Letters from Lea

*A story based on, and including,
actual letters written in 1932 and 1933*

Written by Terry Létienne

Foreword by Joe Mahy

Terry L

◆ FriesenPress

Suite 300 - 990 Fort St
Victoria, BC, V8V 3K2
Canada

www.friesenpress.com

ISBN
978-1-4602-8731-6 (Hardcover)
978-1-4602-8732-3 (Paperback)
978-1-4602-8733-0 (eBook)

1. BISAC code 001

Distributed to the trade by The Ingram Book Company

To my dad Maurice and to my uncle Jean—
though your lives have taken different paths,
there is quite a bit of Lea in both of you.

Joe Mahy

To my grandparents, who died long before
I was ever able to really get to know them.

Terry Létienne

v

FOREWORD

When do we begin to realize the importance of family members who came before us? How do actions taken by our ancestors many years ago affect our lives today?

When I was ten, I learned that Dad had a box of letters that he had received from Uncle Jean. The letters were written in 1932 and 1933 by their mother, Lea, while she was a patient at Souris Hospital in southwestern Manitoba. The letters were written to her husband, Louis, my grandfather, and to her mother, Sylvie Charles.

The letters were written in French, and, since I did not speak the language, I wasn't able to read them on my own. My parents speak both English and French, so occasionally we would take the letters out and Mom would translate one or two of them for us. For the most part, the letters remained untouched, left in the original box in no particular order, and my family rarely discussed their contents.

Life goes on. It wasn't until I was married and my wife Michelle and I had two sons of our own that I got more interested in the letters. Only then did it resonate with me that my grandmother had been so young when she first went into the hospital, just twenty-eight years old. At the time, my uncle Jean was two and a half years old, and my father Maurice was only five months old. For the first time in my life, I began to wonder how my grandparents coped with the situation of not knowing when or if their family would ever return to normal.

In the 1930s, my grandparents did not have free health care, they didn't have a telephone or a car, and the gravel roads from Grande Clairière to Souris were poor in the summer and quite often impassable in the winter.

About five years ago, on a visit to my parents, a discussion came up about the letters, and I decided I would photocopy them and have them translated so that this part of my family's history would not be forgotten.

The letters are now over eighty years old. All of them were written in pencil and have become somewhat faded, but are still quite legible. Most of the original envelopes are intact. It wasn't until I leafed through them to photocopy them that I realized how many letters there actually were. And when I read the translation, I realized that Lea's letters told a story that needed to be told.

Letters from Lea brings my grandmother's story to life. Working on this book has allowed me to get to know some of my ancestors without having ever being able to meet them. It has given me insight into what they endured. It showed me how strong and resilient they were, and it gave me a glimpse of my grandparents and how they passed on similar traits to their children. Dad, I can now see where you get your strong will and independence. Uncle Jean, I now know where your compassion comes from and why you love writing letters.

Thank you, Grandma Lea, for leaving us with this beautiful legacy. For many years now, I've wished that I would have known you... now I feel as though I do.

Joe Mahy

...

I am a great believer of things happening for a reason. There is a reason I waited so many years to start writing my first book... I always felt that it had to be the right story, told at the right time. *Letters from Lea* is that story.

These letters tell the tale of a young mother torn from her husband and two young children due to illness. They depict heartache and despair, but reveal so much more. This is a story that gives us a look at life in the 1930s, the state of medical care at that time, and life in the midst of a depression, all with rural Manitoba as the backdrop.

I was honoured to be asked to translate these letters, and feel privileged to have been given the opportunity to expand on them and piece together a version of this untold tale. Thank you to the Mahy family for trusting me to tell this remarkable story.

Terry Létienne

"Family faces are magic mirrors. Looking at people who belong to us, we see the past, present and future."

Gail Lumet Buckley

CHAPTER 1
October 1928

As she headed towards the general store, Lea felt the chill of the north wind sting her face. She darted across the large clearing near her home. She was glad to reach the small bluff of trees about a mile down the road. Though the branches were barren, the trees still provided some protection from the wind. This was the only shelter she would find until she reached Grande Clairière, a small village in southwestern Manitoba. By the time she arrived at the edge of town, Lea was downright cold. She began to run.

October generally had some warm and sunny days in this part of the country, but not this year. The last few days had been unusually cold, and it had been well over a month since the first overnight frost, when she and *Maman* had had to quickly pull the remaining vegetables from the garden, along with whatever Seneca root they could still find growing in the wild. Frost was a sure sign that winter was on its way.

Lea began to sprint. Her long, lanky legs allowed her to make great strides in a short amount of time. Once she arrived in the town's centre, she glanced briefly to where Anna Hardy lived, but saw no signs of activity. Mrs. Hardy was the mother-in-law of Lea's best friend, Nora, and Nora often spent afternoons helping Anna do yard work. Lea thought they must be inside; it was just too cold to be doing any work outdoors. As she passed by Cyrille and Rosalie Delaite's house, she caught a glimpse of the elderly couple standing outside near their front porch. Both waved to her. Rosalie was a good friend of her fiancé's mother. Soon, she would be her neighbour. For a quick moment, Lea admired the tiny house behind the Delaite's, where she and Louis would be residing. One more month until their wedding day; she couldn't wait.

Lea reached the town's only church, where she and Louis would soon be making their vows, and veered right, heading quickly towards the general store, one of the few businesses in the entire town. By the time she arrived, her nose was runny and her face was stinging from the cold. She could barely feel her toes. She entered briskly, closing the heavy wooden door tightly behind her.

Pallard's general store was a hub of activity. Here, one could pick up a number of dry goods and sundries. It was the place to purchase tickets for either of the daily

Canadian National Railway trains that passed through. The rail line and shelter was just a half mile up the road. The store owner, François Pallard, a tall, thin man with muscular arms, was also the postmaster, so he would pick up the mail and parcels from the train three times a week. Regardless of the type of job he had, M. Pallard was always dressed in formal attire—most times a white, neatly pressed shirt, a grey and burgundy paisley necktie, grey pants and a black wool vest.

Lea had ventured out to pick up a few baking ingredients so that she could make some butter tarts. She also hoped that her package from Winnipeg had arrived in the mail.

"Bonjour, M. Pallard," said Lea as she stepped beside the counter, happy to feel the warmth from the burning coal.

"Bonjour, Mademoiselle Charles," replied M. Pallard, as he twiddled his bushy brown beard. "You must be here to pick up your mail," he said, and he reached into the wooden mail slot behind him, pulling out a stack of stamped envelopes.

"Well, yes, I am… but I was also hoping that my Eaton delivery had arrived."

M. Pallard rummaged through the packages the train had dropped off the previous day. Lea surmised that he must have gained the strength in his arms by lifting all those parcels off the train.

"Here it is," he said as he picked up a box wrapped in dark blue and white wrapping. "You seem quite excited. Is this something special?"

"Oui, M. Pallard. This is my wedding dress!"

M. Pallard flashed a wide grin and nodded. He rang up Lea's items on his new McCaskey cash register—flour, baking powder and currants for a total of eighty-seven cents—and placed them into the knapsack Lea had brought with her. He then handed her the package from Winnipeg. "Voila, ma fille!"

Lea spent a few minutes warming up by the stove before heading outside once again. She chatted with a few other townsfolk and then headed back to the farm. On the way home, she felt positively giddy about finally receiving her wedding dress. How silly, she thought. It is just a dress.

But with less than a month until her wedding to Louis Mahy, she was glad the package had finally arrived. She had found the dress in person at Eaton's, Winnipeg's biggest department store, when she and Maman had taken a two-day trip earlier in the year.

They had chosen a time in early July, when the garden was well-established, but not yet in need of picking. This way, they could spend a few days away without too much worry. They took the train from Grande Clairière to the big city, with stops along the way in Hartney, Elgin, Minto, and Dunrea to pick up passengers. The train rode past the town of Ninette, where they got a quick glimpse of the Ninette Sanatorium, the fine group of buildings that had been built especially for those suffering from tuberculosis. Lea wondered as they passed by the site... if Louis' two sisters had been treated there, would it have been enough to save them? She had heard it was a beautiful facility that provided excellent care. With the delay at the Hartney Junction, just three miles out of Belmont, where a few freight cars were added to the line and the train switched tracks, the trip took a long time, nearly four hours. But it was well worth it.

Lea and her mother arrived in Winnipeg mid-afternoon, at the grand CNR station on Main Street. This magnificent building, designed by the same architects as the Grand Central Station in New York City, featured a huge dome painted a deep blue with molding gilded in gold leaf. As they stepped out the front doors of the grand building, they eyed the towering, glitzy Fort Garry Hotel on Broadway. It was much taller than a grain elevator, but not nearly as tall as the skyscrapers popping up all over New York that they had seen in magazines. What made this building spectacular is that it was so ornate. It really was a sight to be seen. Built by the Grand Trunk Pacific Railway in 1913, the Fort Garry was chateau-style, twelve stories high, built of grey limestone brick and copper roofing. Its rooms were said to be state-of-the-art, most having their very own indoor plumbing. Sylvie and Lea had thought of staying there for two nights, but it was just too rich for their pocket-books. Instead, they chose to stay with family friends from Grande Clairière who had recently moved to Saint-Boniface. Their friends' home was a nice walk away from Winnipeg's downtown, was free of charge, and gave them time to visit with old friends.

Winnipeg was a bustling city. As they walked north on Main Street from the train station, they marvelled at the sheer number of people on the street and in the city streetcars. They had considered taking a ride in one, but it was such a nice, sunny day that they decided to walk instead.

The Provencher Bridge was less than a mile away. They turned onto Water Avenue and made their way to the pedestrian walkway over the Red River to the city of Saint-Boniface. The bridge was built of bright green metal and seemed to tower above the water. As they walked across, they couldn't help but notice how noisy the streetcar was as it barreled across in the centre of the bridge. Once they crossed the bridge, they headed south onto rue Taché, walked past and admired the breathtakingly beautiful Cathédrale de Saint-Boniface, and a short walk later, turned onto rue Despins and down the street until they found their friend's home.

They spent a lovely evening with friends, feasting on paté de fois gras and bread, sipping wine, listening to music on the family's new gramophone, and playing a few games of five hundred.

The next morning, they crossed over Saint-Boniface's famed bridge once again and then headed to noisy, busy Portage Avenue, where the Eaton's building was located. The T. Eaton Company was an impressive place. It featured eight floors of retail, filled with everything imaginable. Patrons accessed the various floors by escalator—an actual moving staircase—or by elevator, where an operator greeted you as you entered the lift. Both were quite the treat for Lea and her mother. Escalators and elevators were nowhere to be found in or around Grande Clairière.

The third floor had a huge "groceteria" with more choices than Lea and her mother had seen in their entire lives. It was a wonderland. They could have so easily spent hours on that floor alone, but they were there for one thing, and one thing only.

The purchase of a wedding dress seemed like such a huge expense to Lea. Luckily, Maman had offered to pay for her dress in return for help at home. Lea was the last one of the girls in her family to get married, and, now in her mid-twenties, she had remained at home much longer than her older sisters ever had. Besides, her mother had the means to pay for it. Times were good on the farm, and Maman's side ventures were also doing well.

Normally, Lea sewed her own clothes. Maman had taught her well and Lea had a knack for it. But this was her wedding dress, and she wanted it to be special… a store-bought dress. Being a winter wedding, Lea had her

heart set on a simple wool dress—not frilly or extrava-
gant like those she saw in fashion magazines—just a
plain wool dress, calf length, or just below the knee. The
beautiful pearls Louis gave her for her birthday would
be more than enough to add elegance. She had already
decided that she didn't want a fancy veil or a lacy,
intricately-decorated hat… maybe just a small white silk
flower at the side of her coiffed hair.

It didn't take long for Lea to find the dress she wanted.
She wasn't fussy like most other girls. Perhaps it was
because she was a little older and wiser than most other
brides-to-be. At the age of twenty-four, Lea was almost
a spinster. It's not that she hadn't had gentlemen suitors.
She just hadn't been about to marry the first man that
came along. She had been fine living on the farm alone
with Maman. But then Louis had come along. He was
the only man who really swept her off her feet. He was
handsome and charming. Even though he was a man
of few words, Lea and Louis had great conversations
about everything under the sun. She loved how witty he
could be and she always laughed at his unabashed sense
of humour.

Once Lea's measurements were taken and the dress
was ordered, the two women enjoyed a light lunch in the
Grill Room on the fifth floor of Eaton's. They ordered the
quaintest little sandwiches served on fine bone china and
shared a piece of delicious red velvet cake.

Then, with time to spare before heading back to Saint-Boniface for one more evening, they completely indulged themselves by getting facials. Maman carried with her a newspaper clipping that indicated these treatments were on sale that day for one dollar. Although this was fairly expensive, both Maman and Lea agreed it was likely one of the last times they would have such an opportunity. They wanted to make this trip an extra special one.

As the esthetician wrapped hot towels around their faces, Sylvie and Lea chuckled at the frivolity of it all. Afterwards, they compared notes. While at times it had been quite relaxing, they had hated when the esthetician had picked blackheads off from their noses. Neither of them would likely ever have a facial again. Money could be better spent on something more practical.

While at the beauty salon, Lea read an article in the June issue of *Chatelaine* called "Advice to those about to enter Matrimony—As the Chatelaine Sees It" and smiled at the contents of the article. The main piece of advice was to learn how to cook well and learn the fundamentals of housekeeping. With Sylvie Charles as her mother, Lea had learned these tasks long ago. She was ready.

When Lea returned home from Pallard's store, she immediately smelled the delicious aroma of Maman's *sucre à crème*. She dashed into the kitchen, kissed her mother on both cheeks and proceeded to warm her hands by placing them near the woodstove.

"Maman, my dress has arrived!" she said. Once her hands felt toasty warm, she grabbed the parcel from the kitchen counter, hastily opened the box, pulled the dress out, and held it to her slim frame.

"*Formidable!*" said Sylvie. "You will be a beautiful bride."

"It is perfect. It is exactly what I wanted. I think Louis will like it. Don't you, Maman?"

Sylvie smiled as she saw the look on her daughter's face and the twinkle in her eyes. She couldn't help but think at that moment that Lea resembled her when she was younger. Now, Sylvie was a tad shorter than Lea, likely from a slouch in her back that came on as she aged, and she had grey, curly hair compared to Lea's slightly wavy, black hair. But they definitely had the same blue eyes and massive smile.

Lea leafed through the pile of letters. Two were addressed to her mother, one from Lea's older sister, Marie, in Eastend, Saskatchewan, and another from a relative in Belgium. Two were addressed to Lea. One was from her niece, Louise, also in Eastend, and another from Louis' brother, who lived in Dollard, Saskatchewan. All were likely responses to their wedding invitations.

The last letter was from the Manitoba Department of Education. Lea wondered if this response would finally bring resolution to a matter that she and her mother had been trying to resolve for the last two months. She

opened the letter from the Deputy Minister of Education
and began reading.

> In reply to your favor of the 20th instant, I beg
> to say that I wrote Inspector Hunter recently
> and have his reply...saying that he found
> your complaint irregular which means that it
> must be amended. I presume he has written
> you about this...we have instructed Mr.
> Hunter to take up your complaint promptly
> as soon as it has been lodged in proper form
> in accordance with the Act.

Such nonsense. She had hoped that the last letter she
had written to the Deputy Minister of Education would
have finally settled the issue. It all started with a complaint Lea penned on behalf of her mother about the
questionable qualifications of a recently-elected local
school trustee. Proper education was of great importance
to Sylvie, and she wanted to ensure that the children in
the region, which included many of her own grandchildren, were properly served. If Sylvie Charles saw a
wrong, she tried to make it right.

Rather than handle the complaint, the Inspector of
Schools and the Department of Education took issue
with the way the complaint was lodged. Because her
mother was not able to write in English, Lea wrote
the letter for her. A response followed saying that Lea
couldn't file the complaint because she wasn't a rate-
payer. She was told to write the letter for her mother and

then have her sign it, which she did, but then received yet another letter only saying the matter would be dealt with in due course. And now this!

Time to move on, Lea thought. She and Maman were busy enough preparing for her November nuptials. Now that the outside farm work was done, she would much rather fuss over plans for her wedding day than this bureaucratic folly with the Department of Education. Besides, her mother was planning another dance at the house on Friday, and they needed to prepare for that as well. Lea took the baking ingredients out of her knapsack and pulled Maman's ceramic mixing bowl out of the cupboard. Time to start making some butter tarts.

CHAPTER 2

October 1932

Friday, October 21, 1932

Cher Louis,

I'm well enough. I slept through the night for the first time since I've been here. I don't think that I will be able to return home next week, unless things take a turn for the better. How is little Maurice? I am sure that he is no longer thinking of me. And Jean... he must often ask for his mother. Let both mothers know how I am, as I am not able to write for long. Once I can sit up in bed, I will write to let you know when I might possibly go home. If 'la mère' hasn't sent her Eaton's order yet, could you ask her to buy me ten pounds of Santos coffee? It's on sale this week for $2.55.

*That's all for today. A big kiss to Jean
and Maurice.*

*Your little wife,
Lea Mahy*

*PS. I ate yesterday for the first time since
I've been here—a bit of clear soup. No
bread though.*

Lea Mahy had been in Souris Hospital for nearly a
week. She had been brought there with severe pain in
her abdomen and was diagnosed with appendicitis.
The doctor in Souris immediately operated on her, and
the surgery seemed to have gone well. Now she was
supposed to be recuperating, but something just didn't
feel right.

As she lay in bed, her stitches throbbing and a dull
pain in her abdomen, Lea thought back to the day she
had been whisked from her home in Grande Clairière.
The morning of October 17 began as most others, with
the whimpering sound of her youngest child, Maurice,
just as daybreak arrived. He was undoubtedly ready for
another full day of food, fun and frolic. As she pulled
herself out of bed to reach him, an ache swept across her
stomach in what could only be described as a sensation
as severe as a labour pain. Lea set herself back down on
the bed and reached her hand across the other side, only
to find there was no one there. Louis had left for the
day already.

Before Lea could make her way to Maurice, two-year-old Jean was already standing by the crib, trying to console his baby brother by handing him a toy rattle. Thank goodness, she thought. Already at the tender age of two, Jean knew how to tend to his sibling. Lea sat up slowly, paused a few seconds and then stood up on the chilly wooden floor. What was this constant pain she was feeling? She'd had this before—many times, in fact—ever since Maurice was born, but this time it was worse.

She made her way to the baby, lifted him, and headed to the kitchen where she could give the boys a bite to eat. She tore open a bag of soda crackers and picked up some applesauce from the kitchen shelf. As she opened the jar, the aroma made her nauseous. She looked down at her stomach. It was completely bloated, as though she were expecting another child. Something was terribly wrong. She felt the need to go to her mother's house, where she could have some of Maman's medicine. That would settle her stomach and make her feel better. There, she and her boys could be in the care of a woman who would know what to do.

Maman's house was three miles away. Lea knew that she could not muster the strength to walk there with the children in tow. She decided to go ask for help from her neighbour, Anna Hardy. Hopefully, her good friend Nora would be there, and if her husband Pierre was not working, he could take Lea to Maman's with his horse-drawn cart.

With great effort, Lea slipped on a blue linen dress and a chenille sweater and dressed the boys in some play clothes. She made her way next door, carrying baby Maurice and holding on tightly to Jean's tiny hand. She was relieved that there was no snow on the ground yet. That could have impeded any attempts to carry the baby while she was in such pain. Still, it was chilly, even with the early morning sun peeking through the clouds on the horizon. The beginning of a long prairie winter was definitely in the air. For a split second, she thought about the need to pull the remaining potatoes from the ground before the first snowfall arrived. I must remember to do this as soon as I return home, she reminded herself.

The rest of that day was a blur for Lea. She barely recalled arriving at her neighbour's door, or being tended to by Nora and Anna Hardy, while Pierre prepared the horse and buggy. She had just a fading memory of the uncomfortable ride to her mother's house and the morning she spent there. She did not know until much later that Dr. Riddell, the local doctor from Hartney, had made a house call early that afternoon. She was barely conscious when he took her on a thirty mile journey to Souris Hospital in his own vehicle. What she did remember vividly was Jean's wailing cry as she was being carried away from Maman's front porch.

So here it was, a week later, and Lea was still being told by Louis that poor, sweet Jean cried often, asking for her every single day. Lea's heart ached at the thought of it. Maurice, a cute, pudgy baby with a cheery disposition, was only five months old. Thankfully, he soon settled in with his new caregiver, his Grandmaman. In a way, that was consoling to the young mother.

Lea found it odd that one minute she would be distraught about her situation, but then the next minute, she would be thinking pragmatically about her role as wife and mother. There was a house to tend to and lots to prepare before winter arrived. The boys were both growing so fast and would soon need some new clothes. Lea had already purchased a new Butterick pattern and the necessary material to sew some winter pants for her young boys. Just as her mind raced from practical to melancholy thoughts, so did her convalescence sway back and forth... one day hopeful, the next day discouraging. As a hundred things ran through Lea's mind, she leaned to her side table and turned out the coal lamp so she could try to get some sleep.

Chère Maman,

A few words to tell you that I am well enough, but it is a long road to healing. Who would have thought that we would be in such a predicament when I left you? I am sure that you must be very tired at times. It would be so nice

*if I were able to return home. The way things
are going, I am not counting on this, as healing
seems to be taking its time. It is frustrating that
you have not been able to visit me. Give Jean
and Maurice hugs for me. My poor little ones, I
miss them so much.*

Your daughter who loves you,
Lea

On the morning of October seventeenth, when a
horse-drawn cart had approached her front door, Sylvie
Charles thought perhaps one of her children, or possibly a grandchild, was coming by for a visit, albeit a bit
early in the morning. She was quick to open the door to
greet them. When she saw the grimace on her daughter's face however, she knew immediately that something
was amiss.

Sylvie's motherly instinct swept over her. She had
Pierre Hardy carry Lea to a room upstairs, where her
daughter could have a quiet place to rest. She gave her
two teaspoons of her homemade tonic, made of raspberries, vanilla, horehound and Seneca root, hoping
this would ease the pain. Sensing this was much more
than just a stomach ache, she arranged for Pierre to take
a note to Dr. Riddell in Hartney, a town twelve miles
away, who made a house call that very afternoon. After a
thorough examination, he suggested that Lea be brought
to the hospital in Souris as soon as possible. In fact, he
drove her there himself.

Sylvie garnered the help of one of her granddaughters, Marguerite Copet, to watch over Jean and Maurice. She then made her way into town, and to the general store, where she could call the store in the town of Bernice, some ten miles away. Louis was there helping his brother Léon with the last of his farm work before winter. She hoped that she could reach someone there who could track Louis down. Sylvie knew how important it was to contact Louis. He needed to get himself to Souris to be with his wife as soon as possible. Luckily, she was able to reach him by late afternoon.

At sixty-eight years old, Sylvie Charles still had energy and vitality. She knew that she could look after Lea's young brood for as long as was necessary until her daughter's health improved. She knew that she was the most sensible choice to take care of Jean and Maurice. Louis' and Lea's siblings were just too busy with young families of their own. As she watched her daughter being taken away to the hospital that afternoon, she just wished she could take away the pain that had doubled her daughter over.

Less than a week later, when Sylvie read her first letter from Lea, sadness swept over her. There was no way she would be able to get to Souris Hospital any time soon to visit her daughter. A huge storm had dumped over two feet of snow across the prairies, and the drifts made many roads impassable. She had heard from Louis about the excruciating pain Lea had undergone, even though her daughter did not allude to much discomfort in her letter. She understood her daughter's sorrow at not being able to spend time with her young children. Mostly, she was upset because after this very serious operation, Lea's prognosis was still unclear.

October 28, 1932

Cher Louis,

I continue to feel better. I am no longer suffering, but you would not believe what I've endured. I thought that I would return home next week, but the doctor told me that I need to be confined to the bed until the 6th of November. So, as you can see, I have more to go through for the moment. In the meantime, I miss you and the boys. I wish I could have Jean and Maurice with me, if only for one minute.

Did you speak to the doctor when you were last here? He told me that this was a worse appendicitis attack than he originally thought. My wounds are still leaking. Some days are worse than others. Write me to tell me how the boys are doing. Also, when you come and get me, do not forget to bring my overshoes. The priest's helper arrived yesterday. She was also operated on and is now placed next to me, but we haven't been able to talk to each other yet.

Give Jean and Maurice big hugs and kisses for
me... and of course hugs and kisses to you too.

Your little wife,
Lea Mahy
Souris Hospital

In the four years that they had been married, Louis
had never seen Lea in such a state. Generally, of the two
of them, Lea was the healthy one. She barely ever caught
a cold or flu, and even when she was down with something, she never complained and trudged through caring
for the children or cleaning the house. In good times
and in bad, in sickness and in health... these words had
so much more meaning now. Louis couldn't get the last
image of his wife out of his head: lying in a hospital bed,
pale and listless, her wounds gaping through bandages
soaked in blood.

Lea was also the optimistic one. When things went
wrong, she always saw the light at the end of the tunnel.
She often told Louis that any setbacks were meant to
be, because a lesson could be learned from them. Soon
after they were married, Louis began to work for the
Canadian National Railway, helping to maintain rail
lines in Manitoba and Saskatchewan. That had him
working many long days for nearly a year. Some nights,
he would not come home at all. Lea did not like that
Louis was away from home that much, but rarely complained about it.

"We will keep in touch by writing to each other," she told him. "It will be fun." But then, that wasn't always possible, because Louis was rarely at one destination for any length of time. Still, Lea reassured him that things would one day get better. And, just as she said, things did get better. Before long, Louis' work was often much closer to home, and he was home in time for supper most every night.

A few years after they were married, Lea gave birth to their first child—Jean Louis Mahy. He was born at the place Louis and Lea now called home, a small municipal property that was rented out to locals. It was a small one-storey with three rooms—a living room, a kitchen and a bedroom. It was on a decent sized lot, which was great for gardening, and it had a recently-built outhouse. The biggest advantage was that it was right in the centre of town. This was good for Louis, who needed to be close to the train station when railroad work was offered to him. And before long, they were expecting their second child. Maurice Pierre Mahy was born at Grandmaman Charles' house in May, 1932.

And so, Louis and Lea had their own home and had started their own little family. Times were tough. After all, it was the early 1930s and the depression was starting to take hold in Canada. Louis did not always have regular work with Canadian National, but he also helped local area farmers wherever he could. Lea actually preferred it when Louis was not on track maintenance, because that meant the couple could spend more time together. Lea continually encouraged Louis to remain optimistic about finding permanent work and about life in general. They loved being together and they cherished their two darling little boys. They looked forward to better times and possibly expanding their family.

CHAPTER 3

November 1932

November 4, 1932

Cher Louis,

I am still bedridden and I don't know for how much longer. The priest came to visit us yesterday and he said he would be back on Tuesday with Rosalie. Maybe you can get a car ride with them and come as well. In the end, it's your decision. Jean must often mention the man who came to take away his mother. Maurice likely no longer thinks of me. That is all for today. I await your news.

Hugs to Jean and Maurice,
and of course to you as well,
Lea

On this particular day, Lea felt a tad better than she had in days. She still wasn't able to sit up in bed, but she gathered enough energy to write a brief letter to her husband. Writing was therapeutic for Lea. It allowed her to think of a better time, hopefully in the near future, when she would return home to be with her family.

The days were long and lonely at the hospital. Lea was thankful for the companionship of her roommate, an elderly lady with a tiny frame who was in hospital for complications due to diabetes. Mme. Gauvreau lived in Hartney, and at one time had lived in Grande Clairière, where she'd worked for a number of years as the priest's housekeeper. Lea had only spoken to her a few times during those years, but now, sharing a room together, the two were learning much more about each other's lives.

Lea appreciated Mme. Gauvreau's wisdom and acceptance of her circumstances. The woman had been living for years with an amputated leg, yet she never saw herself as a victim. She moved herself around using crutches and had an interminable strength. Fourteen years earlier, Mme. Gauvreau had lost something much more precious than a limb. Her son Gabriel died at the age of twenty-six from the flu, a victim of the pandemic that had hit the prairies. Nineteen years before that, she had been widowed when her first husband died in an industrial accident. They lived in France at the time with their two young children. Soon after her husband's death, her in-laws, who had immigrated to Canada a year earlier, arranged to bring her and her children to live with them. Later in life, she married for a second time, but had not been able to have any more children. The sixty-two year old was optimistic and cheerful, despite all of the tragedies in her life. She was also caring and offered a sympathetic ear when Lea lamented about missing her young sons.

Both Lea and Mme. Gauvreau were pleased to see Father Bertrand and appreciated that he took the time to drive out from Grande Clairière to visit them. After all, he was braving the cold winter weather that was so prevalent in Manitoba. There had been a few more snow-storms since the huge dumping of snow in late October. Driving on the gravelled roads had become treacher-ous and the graded roads were nearly impassable. The trek from Grande Clairière to Souris was more than twenty-five miles and took well over an hour by car in the winter. If anyone could tackle this type of challenge, though, it would be Father Bertrand. A small man with a big personality, he was a great proponent of automobiles. He wasn't shy to give his opinion, and was convinced that the days of the horse and buggy should be behind them. He encouraged anybody and everybody to get an automobile. He loved driving and had a reputation for driving at high speeds… sometimes as high as forty-five miles per hour. He was known to say that there were only two speeds to drive a car—fast and faster. Lea and her roommate were also happy to hear that Rosalie Delaite, a mutual family friend, would be visiting them in the next week, weather-permitting. Visitors always brought such joy. For a moment, they were able to forget where they were and their sad circumstances.

Lea hoped that she could convince her husband to drive up with Father Bertrand, although she knew that Louis would give the excuse that the priest drove too fast. Louis once accompanied the priest to Winnipeg to help him pick up church goods, and returned to Grande Clairière swearing he would never be in a vehicle with that man again. "Priest or not," he told Lea. "it's sinful the way that man drives. He doesn't slow down for anything, not even in sleet or snow." Louis much preferred to take a train. He wasn't really accustomed to motor vehicles and wondered about their safety, especially once the snow arrived.

Whatever way he chose to travel, Lea yearned for him to visit soon. He usually tried to pay her a visit every three or four days, but with the onslaught of winter, he hadn't been able to get over to see her for well over a week, and she could no longer bear it. She closed her eyes and imagined her husband's face was right in front of her own. How she missed seeing his dreamy eyes and his big, goofy smile. She kept her eyes closed longer still, envisioning her little boys. How she wished she could hold them in her arms again.

Lea could not help but think that her children were probably frightened and confused by her absence. She

was aware that the baby had taken quite well to his
new surroundings and new caregivers. But little Jean...
she knew he was sad and asked for her often. He must
wonder why she'd been away from him for so long. That
thought alone gave her chills. She did not want to dwell
on it too much, as it served no purpose but to cause her
sadness and distress. Instead, she just visualized their
lovely little faces, wishing she at least had a photograph
of them. I must ask Maman to take a picture of them for
me, she thought.

November 9, 1932

Cher Louis,

*A few words to tell you that I am feeling well
enough. Yesterday was awful though, as my
wounds were leaking terribly. There should
soon be an end to this. My stomach is huge.
The man from Hartney, who used to be in a
room downstairs, came to see Mme. Gauvreau
and mentioned that his stomach was also
inflated like this after his operation and that it
was likely just gas.*

*Jean must have been happy to see you return
home. You say the doctor told you that I might
be home for Christmas. We must not count on
this, though.*

*That is all the news I have for now. Kiss the
two dear little ones often for me.*

Lea

PS. Write me a few words.

Time was passing by so rapidly for Louis while Lea
was convalescing. Not long after she was hospitalized,
he was called back to work on the railroad tracks, an
eleven day stretch that meant a decent paycheque at the
end of it. So just two days after Lea's operation, Louis was
putting in long days at work. He barely had time to see
Jean and Maurice before leaving, but he knew they were
in good hands with their grandmother.

Louis hated to leave while Lea was so ill, but as the
breadwinner of the family, he felt he had no choice. The
depression had taken root in the prairies, and when
work came along, you took it. Farmhand jobs were near
impossible to find, especially at this time of year, forcing
Louis to return to his other line of work. He had been
fortunate to get hired by Canadian National in their
maintenance division. It wasn't steady work and it was
often miles away from home, sometimes for up to a
month at a time, but the pay was decent, twenty-seven
dollars per week.

Louis was thankful that Lea had spent so much of
the summer tending to their large garden. She watered
rows upon rows of vegetables with well water and pulled
weeds whenever she could. Her hard work had paid off,

as they now had enough food to keep their family fed for a long while. Drought and dust storms had been prevalent for the last three summers on the prairies, and these conditions were starting to take their toll on Manitoban farms. Luckily, between Lea, her mother, and her sisters, they were able to maintain their gardens and produce enough food to share with each other and to sustain their families for the long winter ahead.

As Louis read Lea's latest letter, he was troubled by the fact that she was still not out of the woods. By now, he thought, she should have been well on the road to recovery from her operation. Instead, she seemed to be encountering one complication after another. He was eager to go back to the hospital and talk to the doctors about the state of her health.

When he read that she thought Jean would be happy to see him, he felt a lump in his throat. His two year old son seldom smiled since his mother had been taken from him. Baby Maurice was too young to understand, but Jean was old enough to know that the prime nurturer in his life was gone, and he cried often. Sometimes, seeing Louis only magnified the reality that his mother was not there. It made Louis think he might be better to stay away from visiting at Sylvie's rather than cause such pain on his young son. At times, nothing could console the child. He must find a way to bring Jean to see his mother, he thought. It would do them both a world of good.

Lea's postscript was challenging for Louis. Her desire was for him to write to her as often as she wrote him. This was difficult for Louis. He didn't have the education that she had, so his writing skills were mediocre at best. He also could not express himself as well as she could. Words came so easily to Lea. He had plenty to say, but thought it best not to let her know what was really on his mind. He didn't want his wife to worry about what worried him.

How were they going to face the financial struggles stemming from Lea's illness? Her medical bills were racking up. How much longer could his mother-in-law look after the boys? After all, though Sylvie seemed to be handling the situation well, and was a very giving person, she was an aging woman. Certainly, over time, being the main caregiver to two toddlers would take its toll. And finally, how long would it be before Lea could come home? And when she did, would they still be able to live there? Louis was starting to think that if Lea's illness lingered, he would not be able to afford to rent the house much longer. His only option would be to give it up and move in with family members in order to pay the bills. These were not thoughts he wanted to share with his dear wife.

He chose to visit Lea in person instead. There was nothing he'd be able to say in writing.

November 11, 1932

Cher Louis,

A few words to give you a bit of news. Everything is about the same. The doctor placed a tube in me again today. The nurse told me that this would make the pus leak out quicker. I asked him again today how long he thinks he needs to keep me in bed and he said he couldn't tell me anything. My stomach is swollen and the doctor said that this is why I'm not healing faster. In the end, we just need to be patient, although I find it very lonely here all alone. Maurice will not recognize me, and Jean... does he still talk about me? That's all for today.

Kisses to you and the two dear little ones,
Your wife, Lea

In one of her conversations with her primary doctor, Dr. Fraser, a tall, intellectual-looking man with a gentle demeanor, Lea found out that he had been practicing at Souris Hospital for eight years. He told her that he had arrived to a less than stellar facility, one with an inadequate operating room and inefficient equipment. He praised the hospital for the recent improvements that had been made, the addition of electric lighting in the main areas of the building, for one, and was thankful for the new superintendent of nurses. She had implemented some new procedures to ensure professional standards were met and cleanliness was maintained. He told Lea that she was in very capable hands, and he and his staff were doing what they could to deal with the post-appendectomy infection she had developed.

Lea had figured out on her own that the surgical wound had become infected. The incision constantly bled and discharged yellowish-brown, smelly pus. The continual insertion of a drainage tube in the abdominal area made Lea clearly aware that something wasn't quite right. This technique *seemed* to improve the situation, but after almost a month, she was still confined to bed rest and was on a very restricted diet.

Dr. Fraser told Lea that he was optimistic that she could recover. He was consistently researching medical literature to better understand what complications could arise with appendectomies following ruptured appendicitis and consulted with experts in this field. He promised Lea that he would treat her with the greatest gentleness.

On the morning of Remembrance Day, as Dr. Fraser repeated the procedure to drain the pus from Lea's abdomen, Lea began to ask questions. Why were her wounds not healing? What were the complications in her case? When could she go home to be with her family? These were all questions Louis normally bombarded the doctor with when he went to Souris, but he wasn't there, so Lea thought it was time she stood up for herself.

Enough was enough. Lea wanted to get better and she wanted to go home.

November 12, 1932
Chère Maman,

I received your letter. Thank you for the box of chocolates. I wanted to save them but the nurses told me that I had to eat them, so I placed the box beside me, and let me tell you, I am eating them quickly. You will have to hurry up and come for a visit if you want to taste them! You will find that my figure has changed greatly. If only these wounds would heal! I often worry about this. You can eat the beans I have stored at home. Even if I get released soon, I will still have enough to last me the entire season.

How are my two dear little ones? I would love to have a photograph of them. This would only allow me to see their adoring little faces on paper, but at least I could see them. Is little Maurice still behaving well? Does Jean still ask for me? Those poor little ones... when will we see each other again?

The abscess seems to be healing, but it is taking a long time. The other wound is still the same. I am waiting for the day when I will have the pleasure to see you in person.

Your daughter who misses you always,
Lea

As Nurse Edna peered into the room of patients Lea
Mahy and Celina Gauvreau, she could see that both
were sound asleep. Finally, she thought. Most nights, she
would hear the two of them whispering until the wee
hours of the night. In many of those instances, she could
hear Lea sobbing and Celina consoling her.

A licensed nurse for five years now, Edna had worked
solely at Souris Hospital since her graduation in 1927.
She liked practicing there because the hospital was in
her home town, so was close to many family members,
and she knew many of the patients that came through
the door. It was a friendly, familiar place, and she was
happy to help people in her own community.

Nurse Edna did not know Lea Mahy or her family.
Prior to Lea's hospital stay, Edna knew that many families in Grande Clairière had emigrated from Belgium,
and though a few of the residents had been hospitalized
from time to time, she never really got to know anyone
from the small southwestern town. Most of the residents
spoke very little English, which made getting to know
any of them quite difficult.

Since Lea's arrival at Souris Hospital, Edna had been
taken by Lea's sweet demeanour and began to befriend
her. Edna empathized with the young mother. Perhaps
it was because, like Lea, Nurse Edna was also the mother
of two young boys. Perhaps it was because on most evenings that Nurse Edna worked, she would see Lea cry
herself to sleep.

Under normal circumstances, there was barely time to get to know patients who were hospitalized. They came in, received the treatment they needed, convalesced, and went home. Those who lingered, those who had an extended stay at the hospital, usually spiralled one way or the other. Edna saw that as a good thing. No attachment. No emotion.

Nurse Edna found it interesting that when patients were admitted to the hospital, the medical professionals were usually able to determine quite decidedly which direction their illness would take them. Some would survive and some would die. It was a fact of life.

Though she considered herself a highly sympathetic person, Nurse Edna would not allow herself to get attached to any of her patients or become overly emotional about a patient's condition, even if she knew them or members of their family. Following her profession's code of conduct, she kept her emotions in check and went about her work, ensuring only that they were receiving proper care.

Today had been a particularly special day. For the first time since she'd been admitted over a month ago, Lea finally ate a little more than usual. She had received a box of Willard's chocolates, beautifully wrapped in a pink satin box, and it was obvious that these were her favourites. Edna seized on the opportunity to encourage her patient to eat, get some calories in her, and hopefully help her gain a bit of weight. Lea was dreadfully thin, and this concerned the young nurse. Dr. Fraser had lifted the restricted diet Lea was on, and Nurse Edna saw no harm in feeding her a few extra sweets.

Edna could not ignore what her heart was telling her. Here was an ailing young woman, a mother of two little boys, who needed her attention, and no one knew just how her illness was going to evolve. One day, she would be sitting up in bed, eating chocolates and giggling. The next, she would be in unbearable pain, or worse yet, faced with new complications. All Edna could do was to try to keep her comfortable.

She tiptoed into the room and went to Lea's bedside. She removed the pink, flowered box of chocolates from the patient's bed, covered Lea with a grey flannel sheet, and with a small, white towel, dabbed a small teardrop from the young mother's cheek.

November 18, 1932

Cher Louis,

I received your letter yesterday and I was very happy to receive a letter from you. I'm quite well. The wounds are leaking less and less. The nurses told me that there are two little holes that need to heal. I feel much stronger than the last time you came, but I don't know when I will be allowed to get up. The doctor told me yesterday that I could maybe get up next week, but he didn't say that this was for certain. My stomach is big like a barrel but they don't seem concerned. It is odd to have such a big stomach but not be in pain. They put me under a lamp, for one hour, twice a day. I am eating well and sleeping well. Today, they took the big spring out of my bed, so now my bed is completely flat. You mentioned that you may come to see me on Monday with Jean and Maurice. Maman may want to come, but don't make extra work for yourselves. We must be patient. I hope that the children are doing well and do not cry too much for their mother. I also hope that in two or three weeks, I can return home to you and the boys.

Pay attention to the potatoes at home, so that they don't freeze. Are you thinking of moving away for the winter? I will not be able to do much of anything when I get home. I may not be able to take care of Maurice by myself, because he is just too heavy.

Kisses to you and the little ones,
your wife who loves you,
Lea

For the first time in over a month, Louis felt hopeful. By the tone of the letter, Lea finally seemed to be recovering from her operation. Maybe she would make it home in time to prepare for Christmas after all. Maybe she could sew new winter outfits for the boys, as she had planned to do before this whole medical situation arose. He was so pleased that she was eating well and sleeping through the night, and he was especially glad to hear that she was no longer in pain.

Louis poured himself a cup of coffee from the pot that sat on the woodstove. He sat down on a wooden kitchen chair and looked around at the house that they now called home. He thought back to how shabby the place was when they first got it. The walls were stained with dirt, the floors were grimy, and the place had a musty smell. He remembered how quickly Lea was able to transform it. She had thoroughly scrubbed the lath and plaster walls, and when she realized that the dirt would not come off, she ordered some bargain wallpaper from Winnipeg and covered the walls in the living room, kitchen and bedroom. She, her oldest sister Roseanna, and her mother spent days at it, but it was well worth the effort.

After they were done, the house looked amazing. Each room had its own colour scheme—light brown and salmon colours in the living room, yellow and orange in the kitchen and various shades of blue in the bedroom. Lea found some fabric scraps on sale in the department store in Hartney, enough to sew some white lace curtains for the kitchen, and room-darkening ones for the bedroom, and some brightly coloured cushions to place on the sofa. She also found a few picture frames in Maman's shed to hang on the walls. One was of a team of horses pulling a large sleigh in a serene winter landscape; the other was a needlepoint image of a floral bouquet. The end result was a charming and pleasant home with just the right touches.

To think, I actually thought of giving this place up, Louis thought to himself. Now, with Lea's health returning, Louis hoped that they would not have to cross that bridge.

Even though they were renting, Lea and Louis felt an incredible attachment to their house. They loved lounging on their rickety old sofa. Every evening after supper Louis would lie down on it and watch the boys play on a patch-quilted blanket on the floor while Lea cleaned up the supper dishes. When she was done, she would snuggle her way in and lie down beside Louis. Quite often, the little ones would then join in, and before you knew it, all four would be on the couch together, squished on top of each other, and not necessarily comfortable. It was such fun! The boys would laugh hysterically when one of the adults fell off the couch, usually their father. This became a ritual almost every evening until the boys were put to bed.

Not long after they moved in, they had discussed the idea of talking to the municipality about the possibility of buying the house. As long as Louis worked for the railway, he could qualify for a mortgage from Grande Clairière's Banque Nationale. This location was ideal for them. It was right in town, close to the train station and had a large yard with plenty of room for the children to play and a stable to be built, if they ever decided to purchase hens, cows or horses. Of course, the depths of the depression and Lea's illness side-saddled that dream, but they loved the place nonetheless.

Louis thought he should let Lea know that he was doing his best to keep the house clean so she would have a decent place to convalesce when she came home. He wanted her to know how much he longed to lie on the sofa again with his wife and his young sons.

He wondered if it would be possible to bring the boys to see Lea on his next visit. Winter had already come in with a vengeance, and it didn't seem to be letting up. He hoped the next week would bring warmer days. He and Sylvie could then perhaps take Jean and Maurice to see their mother by train. Sylvie had yet to visit Lea in Souris, and Lea would be so happy to see them all. Louis wasn't expected to get another work assignment for at least another week, leaving him time to possibly see Lea on a weekday. Railroad track maintenance was scarce as the weather deteriorated, but Louis was confident that this would pick up again in the new year.

Knowing he didn't have to get up early for work the next day, Louis headed over to the town pool hall to chat with the men and have a beer or two.

November 20, 1932

Cher Louis,

*Again a few words to give you some news...
Your mother must have told you that I was cut
in two areas...one wound is healing better than
the other... the matron of the nurses told me
that if my health stayed the same or improved
slightly, I would be better in no time. The girl
from Hartney, the one who was operated eight
days ago, is going home tomorrow. The doctor
asked that her mother come to get her. I wonder
if he will do the same thing for me. So Jean is
still talking about me after all this time? Those
poor little ones, I never thought that I would
have to leave them for this long. The nurses tell
me that I am gaining weight a little every day.
I can tell by my hands. They are not as thin as
they used to be. I received a letter from Nora.
She asked me if I wanted any books to read. If
you see her or Pierre, tell them not to bother
as I don't read a lot. I will not write to them as
I don't write a lot either lately, because it tires
me. I am sure you must find the time long, but
you have to be strong. We must continue to
have hope that we can be happy again.*

*Sending you hugs and kisses from far away,
wishing I could be close to you again.
Your wife Lea*

From her hospital bed, Lea could barely peer through the window on the other side of the room. What she could see was that the sky was clear blue and the sun was shining brightly, though she knew all too well that looks could be deceiving. It was likely another brisk, freezing day in November on the prairies.

Lea glanced at the calendar on the wall and realized that in two days, she and Louis would be celebrating four years of marriage. She hoped that she would see Louis on the twenty-second to celebrate their anniversary, but then thought how unlikely that would be. Though he didn't have regular work with the railway, when he was called, it was usually mid-week, so it was unlikely he would get to Souris on a Tuesday. He did manage to get a ride, either by car or sleigh, to Souris each Sunday, from the parish priest, a friend, or a family member. Lea was thankful that she saw her husband on a regular basis. If only she could see her children as much.

She wondered if Louis or Maman had picked the last of the potatoes in the garden. There were enough there to last the entire winter. She hoped that none had gone to waste. She thought it best to remind Louis to haul them inside before they spoiled with freezing temperatures. Lea had picked most of the other vegetables in September, and all the canning had been done for the winter ahead. She had canned tomatoes, beans, pickles and onions. All in all, there was a lot of food for her little family, and she was happy about that.

Though Lea was an avid reader and loved to write, most days she could not muster the strength to try either. Once a week, a volunteer from the hospital would come by with a number of books and magazines, and every time, Lea would borrow one of each. The last book she took was an English copy of Victor Hugo's *Les Misérables*, Volume I. She had read the French novel years ago, and thought it might help the time pass if she now read this version. She picked it up once or twice in the last week, but never got past the first page. She looked over at her side-table and saw the gold bound book sitting atop four other books and two copies of the *Ladies Home Journal*. She thought she best hand them all back to the volunteer when she next came to visit.

At times, Lea found the days long and dull, although conversations with Mme Gauvreau helped to pass the time. Mme. Gauvreau had a good listening ear and often let Lea ramble on about her children, how she missed them so, and how they must have grown so much since she last saw them. Her elderly roommate also had some wise words for her. "No sense in worrying," she would tell Lea, in her calm, soft-spoken voice. "Worry will set you on a path you don't want to travel. You just have to have faith that everything is fine. Your boys are fine. Your mother raising them is fine. All is fine."

Having visitors was always a treat, but not many of her relatives and friends were able to get to Souris from Grande Clairière. Whenever she heard footsteps down the hall, Lea would try to sit up in her bed, anticipating that a visitor was heading in her room. Who would it be? Louis? One of her sisters? Maman? Usually, it was one of the nurses or doctors.

Most of Lea's days were filled only with thoughts of home. When would she finally be able to see her boys again? How were they managing without her? How was Maman handling the extra workload of looking after two toddlers? How was Louis handling the extra stress of keeping up with housework, working and taking the time to be with his sons? But sometimes Lea caught herself and remembered Mme. Gauvreau's words.

She sensed that Louis was upset when he last visited her. He barely said a word, but his facial expression was quite telling. She just knew he was troubled about many things. Certainly, this medical setback was tough on him financially. Though he didn't say it, Lea suspected that he might be thinking of giving up the house to help to pay medical expenses. Lea understood the agonizing reality that if things didn't improve soon, losing the house was a definite possibility. And as difficult as it would be, Lea knew that this was a decision in their own best interest. The boys were already living with Maman. Louis could perhaps go live with his brother Léon, who had recently moved his family closer to Grande Clairière, where they had purchased two quarters of land and a house that was only two miles from the Charles homestead. For Lea, just the idea of breaking up her family was upsetting. She tried not to dwell on these sad realities and shifted her thoughts to happier ones. No sense in worrying.

Lea remained optimistic that she was going to go home soon, certainly well before Christmas. She leafed through the Eaton's catalogue and found some items that might be suitable for her boys. She'd found a toy truck for Jean, a pop-up book for Maurice, and some flannel material to sew pyjamas for each of them. Perhaps it was still early enough to order this before the festive season. She looked at her left wrist out of habit, trying to determine the time. She must ask Louis to bring her watch on his next visit.

November 21, 1932

Ma chère Lea,

We too find the time long. We must be brave. We weighed the two little ones on Thursday. Jean weighs thirty-two pounds. Little Maurice weighs twenty-one pounds. As you can see, the boys are doing well with their grandmother. We have a lot of snow, but it is not too cold.

I am sending you some canned goods and a bag of goodies. We are hoping for your return. The little ones are very good. Jean still cries for you but not as much as before. He still speaks often about his mother, even as I write this letter. He also asks his father when you will

be coming home, and Louis tells him that you
will be back one day. Little Maurice is eating
porridge each morning and one or two soda
biscuits in soup at lunch time. At supper time,
he eats macaroni. He is very well-behaved.

Your mother,
Sylvie Charles

Sylvie Charles was a strong, tenacious woman. She
and her husband Joseph had been two of the first inhab-
itants of Grande Clairière, Manitoba, after immigrating
to Canada from Charleroi, Belgium in 1888. At the time,
they had two children—Ferdinand and Georges—who
were both under two years old. The six-week excur-
sion to Canada by boat was horrendous, as Sylvie was
with child once again and felt terribly ill throughout the
entire voyage. Furthermore, her brother and sister-in-
law's baby died on board, likely of cholera, and had to be
buried at sea.

The early years in their new country were demanding for Joseph and Sylvie. They arrived in Oak Lake,
Manitoba with just a few dollars. Just a month after their
arrival, Sylvie gave birth to their first daughter, Roseanna.
Soon, Joseph found work with a local farmer, and eventually, they saved enough money to buy a homestead in
the Grande Clairière area. There, they built a sod house
and began farming.

Over a span of eighteen years, Sylvie would bear nine
more children. Lea and Palmyre were the two youngest,

born in 1904 and 1906 respectively. Joseph and Sylvie eventually built a two-story, wood-framed house on the same land to make room for their growing family. They farmed and made a good living. Joseph was a good carpenter and built solid wood bed frames for the children and a large kitchen table made of oak. Sylvie meticulously sewed curtains and made quilts for each of the bedrooms. It wasn't long before the back porch was converted to a kitchen pantry and filled with fresh vegetables and canned goods.

Sylvie was extremely hard-working and resourceful. She spent most of her days cooking, cleaning and doing laundry for her large family. While most people used their largest pot for stews, Sylvie used hers to cook side-dish vegetables. She used her steel canning pot to boil potatoes, and sometimes had to use two cast iron pots to cook meat for one meal. She established a system for laundry, hand washing clothes in spurts over four days—Joseph's clothes on Monday, her sons' clothes on Tuesday, the girls' clothes on Wednesday, and towels, bed sheets and blankets on Thursday. If one of the children took ill, or something else needed her attention, the whole system would be thrown out of whack. In the summer, aside from her regular chores, she tended to a large garden—corn, peas, beans, carrots, potatoes, and many root vegetables. She carted water from the well each morning and watered her crops before the sun became too strong. Her land was chockfull of Seneca root, which she picked often. She then formulated it into medicine and sold it to the locals.

Though Joseph and Sylvie worked well at keeping their home healthy and harmonious, the same could not be said for their relationship. Unhappy differences caused Sylvie to separate from her husband after thirty-five years of marriage. She remained in the family home, kept and maintained the land, held onto the farm animals and equipment, and continued to raise their three youngest children—Bertha, Lea and Palmyre—on her own. She supported herself with farming and midwifery. She delivered many babies in Grande Clairière and surrounding areas, and eventually taught her daughter Alice to do the same. Rumor was that she also dabbled in making home brew with one of her brothers and two of her sons.

Once she was on her own, away from the demands Joseph had on her, Sylvie became much more free-spirited. She always found ways to create fun experiences for her children and other families in Grande Clairière. She was known to have hosted many house parties. Her sons Léon and Emile played the violin; the girls would sing and dance. Tasty homemade treats, such as apple pie, bread pudding, sucre à crème, and her famous grand-pères au sirop d'érable were always provided.

By 1932, most of Sylvie's children were married with children of their own. All had moved out of their childhood

home. She lived alone, though she was rarely by herself.
Most of her children still lived in the Grande Clairière
area and stayed in touch regularly. By then, she also had
many grandchildren and a few great-grandchildren, who
loved to spend time at Grandmaman's. Visitors were
abundant at Sylvie's house.

If anyone was fit to take care of Louis and Lea's children, it was Sylvie. There were days of late, however,
when she had to drag herself out of bed in the morning
when she heard baby Maurice's cry. The demanding task
of having to care for two boys—both of them babies
really—on a daily basis for well over a month was starting to take its toll. Lately, Sylvie felt a pain in her groin
every time she lifted Maurice. He was a good eater, and
as such, he was growing quickly. Surely his added weight
was causing her to feel this way. She was so thankful
for the help of her granddaughters, Marguerite and
Léontine, who took turns staying with her every day of
the week. Whenever possible, Louis would drop by, play
with the little tykes and help her to put them to bed in
the evenings.

Though Sylvie hadn't had a chance to visit Lea, she
was planning on accompanying Louis on his next visit.
She wondered if she should also bring Jean. Deep down,
Sylvie knew how important it was for Lea to see her children, that it would be the best remedy to keep her spirits
up. She did have a gut instinct however, that it might
not be wise to subject young Jean to the agony of being

separated from his mother once again. As it was, he still cried and asked for her regularly. But, he was slowly getting used to life without her, and seeing her again would only cause his feelings of loss to resurface. Sylvie would have to give this more thought.

In the meantime, she went into the hallway closet and pulled the Kodak box camera she and Joseph had purchased just before they separated. She dressed the two boys in their Sunday best outfits. She brought them to the kitchen, where she dragged a kitchen chair next to the wood panelled wall. She sat baby Maurice on the chair, stood young Jean beside him, and snapped a photograph. It was the last photo taken on this roll of film, which she carefully removed from the camera so that she could ship it to Winnipeg to have it developed. This would make a nice Christmas present for Lea, she thought, whether she was in the hospital or not by that time.

November 21, 1932

Dear Aunty Lea,

I am still staying with Grandma and I am glad to do so. Maurice and Jean know me as well as they know Grandma. I fixed the little table and chairs and Maurice sits on the chair now and plays with small toys. Mother and dad are hoping you are well and coming home

*soon. They come to get me each Friday and
bring Léontine. She stays every Saturday and
Sunday. Then dad brings me back on Sunday
evening and Léontine goes back home so she
can go to school. Sometimes when I get up,
Maurice is already awake. He turns his head
around to see if I am coming. When he sees
me, he is so happy.*

*Your niece,
Marguerite Copet*

Lea and her older sister Louisa were six years apart.
Despite their age difference, the two were close. They
had much in common, especially once Lea married.
They shared tips on how to grow a proper garden and
exchanged recipes for canning and baked goods. In
1930, six months after Jean was born, Louisa gave birth
to a little girl, Lillian, and they then had in common
the joys and tribulations of taking care of a young
baby. When Lea took ill, and her mother took Jean and
Maurice under her wing, Louisa was quick to offer help
by volunteering her two oldest daughters, Marguerite
and Léontine, to take turns staying with Grandmaman,
so that she would have someone to help her seven days a
week. Lea was extremely grateful for this, as she knew it
would be a huge help for her mother in coping with the
added workload.

Lea appreciated that her young niece took the time to
write her a letter, and the very day she received it, she

wrote Marguerite back to thank her for all that she and her sister had been doing to help Grandmaman.

It had been more than a month now since she had been admitted to the hospital. How Lea wished that the town of Souris was closer to home. Then, she might be able to see her sons! By the tone of Marguerite's letter, both boys seemed to have adjusted well to their new day-to-day routine. Lea re-read the letter, closed her eyes and imagined what Maurice would look like now that he was already six months old. She envisioned his big blue eyes and enormous smile, and wondered if he was able to sit up by himself now that he was a month older.

December was just around the corner. She hoped and prayed that it would still be possible for her to be with her children in time for Christmas.

November 30, 1932

Cher Louis,

A few lines to let you know that it hasn't been going well for the last few days. The doctor placed a tube in me once again and my stomach is terribly big. It looks like I am going to bust and my temperature is very high. I was doing so well last week and I thought I was recovering, and now, here I am again with my life completely upside down. If this continues I will not be with you in the new year.

Do you think the roads will be good by Sunday? If they are, could you perhaps get a ride here? Write me back to let me know if you can come or not.

Kisses to Jean and Maurice.

The one who loves you so much,
Lea

Try as she might, Lea could not help but be discouraged. She had been in the hospital for almost six weeks, and she felt like she was getting worse, even though she was constantly being told she was getting better. The wounds on either side of her bulging stomach were irritated, partly from the infection itself, she thought, but also from the tubes that were inserted in them to drain the pus. From time to time she experienced flu-like symptoms like nausea and diarrhea, but again, the nurses told her this was nothing to worry about. She yearned to see her husband and her sons, and she wished more than ever that she could go home.

Mme. Gauvreau had taken a turn for the worse and was moved to another part of the hospital. Lea missed spending time with her. For the past month, the elderly lady had been a source of encouragement for Lea, and more importantly, a shoulder to cry on. Now the poor old dear had troubles of her own. Her diabetes was causing further complications, and doctors were contemplating the amputation of her other leg. The strong-willed woman was refusing to have this done. She had been through enough.

Lea was upset with herself for becoming so dispirited. She felt guilty that she had written in her letter to Louis that she may not be home before January. He would not want to hear that, but it was too late to take it back. The nurse had already taken the letter to be mailed.

Perhaps she should pray more, she thought. As it was, Louis' mother would be disappointed in her that she wasn't asking God to help her cope with the strains of her illness. Marie Mahy was a very religious woman with close ties to the local church. She put all her faith in God for such things and believed fervently that there was a reason for everything. She had tolerated much pain in the course of her life, and praying got her through every obstacle she had faced. Just prior to emigrating from Belgium, she had lost a son, Joseph, from tuberculosis. He was only sixteen years old. Her husband, Nestor, died in 1913, just three years after they had arrived in Canada. Then, not long after her husband's death, her two daughters died—Alix in 1916, at the age of seventeen, and Aurélie in 1920, at the age of twenty-two—also from tuberculosis. Losing her children was a terrible cross to bear, but Marie's deep-rooted religious beliefs pulled her through each day.

Marie, or 'la mère,' as Louis and Lea often called her, was a short, stout woman with a gentle demeanour, but she knew how to get her point across. She insisted that her boys go to church on a regular basis and told them to do so in no uncertain terms.

Lea was very close to her own mother, but still found room in her heart for her 'second' mother, Marie Mahy. The two developed a close relationship once Lea married Louis, and could really tell each other anything and everything. Lea always found it remarkable how Marie remained so composed when she talked about the death of her loved ones. They all died well before their time. No doubt her faith in God helped her through some difficult times.

Now, Lea felt she needed to have more faith in God, herself. She needed to believe that she would recuperate from this illness, return home to Grande Clairière, and resume her life with her little family. She jotted down on a piece of paper to remember to ask Louis to bring her rosary beads. She thought about how long ago she had actually used them. She worried that Louis may not find them easily, as they were probably buried under a whole lot of things stuffed into their top dresser drawer.

November 30, 1932

Chère maman,

I am bedridden as always and don't know for how long. They inserted a tube in me

once again. It is very painful and leaking all
the time.

Mme. Gauvreau comes by to see me every
afternoon in her wheelchair. They want to
amputate her other foot but she is refusing.

If you have a chance to come for a visit, could
you bring me another bandage? I would also
like a bag of flour, as I will need some when I
return home (one has to hope). I hope the little
ones are well as always.

Kisses to you, Jean and Maurice,
Lea

Like his mother, Louis also bore the tragedy of losing
his father and siblings in such a short period of time.
He knew that his mother was heartbroken, and for that
reason, when Louis was of age to leave home and start
a family of his own, he chose not to rush into finding a
future bride. He thought it better to stay with his mother
to take care of her and to help out on the Mahy farm. He
did so until his late twenties.

And then he fell in love with Lea. And life was good.
Lea was so full of energy and always had a word to say
about one thing or another. She made life interesting.
She made him laugh. She filled his days with sunshine.
After spending so many years experiencing sadness,
Louis found it refreshing to have such a positive force in
his life.

And then, this operation and all of its complications rocked his stable life. He could see by his wife's letters that she was sick of the pain. Slowly, he could see her positivity deflate. She still cared about others and often asked about her children and the rest of her family in her letters. However, knowing what he knew about Lea, he was certain that she would only ever complain if things were dismal. What was happening? Without Lea by his side, it was difficult to see the light at the end of the tunnel.

CHAPTER 4

December 1932

December 4, 1932

Ma chère Maman,

I received your letter yesterday. You can't imagine how happy I was to hear that the children are behaving well for you. As for me, I am fine, but I don't think I will be returning home next week. The doctor told me that my appendix had burst several hours before I got here and had I waited any longer, I would have died. If only I had come to the hospital earlier, I may have been home by now.

The priest's servant will be allowed to get out of bed this afternoon. The nurses here are very good and treat me well. They give me a good-tasting tonic three times a day, which I am enjoying. Still, I would rather be home with my family. Alas, I must be patient... I am eating three times a day, but not a lot at a time. They never serve meat or potatoes here.

Give kisses to Jean and Maurice and hugs to you too.

Your daughter for life,
Lea

PS. Last night, all I could do was dream about Jean and Maurice, but in this dream, I was not allowed to see them. I cried all night.

Sylvie was tired. Constantly caring for her two young grandsons took a lot of stamina, much more than she ever anticipated. She was appreciative of the help from her daughters and granddaughters, and Louis when he could help. He had been working long days on track maintenance in the last few weeks, which was necessary considering the hospital bills that had to be paid. He tried to keep up with payments as best he could. He had not ever been in a financial position, prior to Lea's illness, to put any real money aside. What little savings they had was now completely depleted.

Sylvie would never want her ailing daughter to know the toll her hospital stay was having on those who loved her the most. Lea had enough anxiety surrounding her family situation. She missed her sons deeply, longed to be back home in Grande Clairière, and her recuperation was going very slowly.

Sylvie thought back to the day Lea showed up on her doorstep so sick and wondered briefly if it would have made any difference if she had sent for the doctor quicker. She fretted about that for a short time, but then thought how useless it was to turn her thoughts to something that could no longer ever be.

Sylvie watched the boys as they sat and played together on the floor of her living room. Calm and content, they were completely enjoying each other's company. For the most part, Jean and Maurice were well-behaved little tykes, and Sylvie was pleased about that.

With Christmas approaching, Sylvie began to consider what gifts she might give to the two little ones. As their main caregiver, Sylvie thought it best if she would see to it that the boys each receive a gift, relieving Lea of the task. Looking in an upper cupboard in the kitchen, Sylvie found some knitting patterns for children's hats and mitts. She would have to devote more of her evening time to knitting, she decided. She also resolved to make a big batch of sausages, so that Lea would have some when she returned home. Sylvie worried that if Lea continued to eat such small portions, she would lose too much weight. As it was, she was not a heavy girl. She would have some of Lea's favourite meat and potato dishes ready for her when she comes home, Sylvie decided.

Sylvie recognized how important it was for Lea to see her children. She knew that even a short visit with her young sons would be enough to invigorate Lea's spirit and give her the will to fight through this illness. Sylvie thought about how she could manage this. The weather had turned extremely cold, so she would have to wait for the days to be warmer. She pondered on how she could get to Souris, and whether or not she could even manage taking both boys by herself. She decided at this point in time, it was more important for Lea to at least see Jean. He consistently asked for his mother. Lea knew this and desperately wanted to comfort him. Sylvie decided that she would talk to Louis. Perhaps he could take Jean with him on his next Sunday visit.

December 9, 1932

Cher Louis,

I received your letter. I am about the same. The abscess is healing, but very slowly. It will take a long time before it closes up completely.

So you tell me that Mary is now married. I believe that it is a year of funny marriages in Grande Clairière. To each his own, I suppose.

I am eating well, but I am still very frail. I suppose that as long as I stay in bed, I will remain weak.

As always, kisses to my dear little ones. Those
poor little boys... when will I have the pleasure
of seeing them again?

Lea, who thinks of you all the time

Louis was making every effort to send Lea letters on a
regular basis. It is what she wanted. But he always found
it challenging. He knew that she was no longer current
on the town news, so he tried as best he could to keep
her up-to-date on who was dating who, who was getting
married and who was with child. He thought best to
keep it light and keep her mind on less serious subjects.

Louis and his mother-in-law discussed the possibility of bringing Jean to Souris to visit with Lea. Now that
Léon and Palmyre were living nearby, Sylvie was certain
that her youngest daughter would gladly look after baby
Maurice, so that Louis, Jean, and Sylvie herself could all
visit Lea in Souris.

They decided that they would head out on the Sunday
before Christmas. They would have to go by horse-drawn
sleigh, however, so it would be completely dependent on
the weather.

As Louis sat in his mother-in-law's kitchen to write
his next letter to Lea, seven month old Maurice crawled
across the floor and tugged at his father's pant leg.
Instinctively, Louis picked him up and looked into his
child's big blue eyes. How quickly the baby was growing
and how sad, Louis thought, that Lea was missing these

pivotal childhood moments. Louis gave his youngest son a hug, put the child back down on the floor, put the pencil down on the table, and went over to the kitchen counter, where he poured himself a glass of home brew.

Once the children were in bed, Louis returned to town on foot. As he walked towards town on this dismally freezing night, he thought about the inevitability of having to give up their home if Lea wasn't out of the hospital by Christmas. Louis just scraped by to make December's rent payment. He shivered for the remainder of the walk.

As he reached the intersection in town, he decided to veer right to the pool hall. The last thing he wanted to do was walk into that lonely, empty house.

A young woman, cloaked in a white cotton dress, is slowly walking down a long, dark hallway. As she looks ahead, she sees a light. She hears voices... laughter... the sounds of children playing. As the voices get clearer and louder, she walks faster. She wants to reach the children. She hears a familiar tone. A man's voice... one that is soothing... loving. She hears them call her name. She walks faster still. Smiling, she calls back to them "I'm here. Wait for me. I'm coming to see you."

As she tries to edge up to the end of the hallway, something is holding her back. It is as though a strong wind has blown in, preventing the young woman from reaching her destination. It is bizarre. She is inside a building, yet, she is walking in a windstorm. The voices begin to fade. The children begin to cry. After what seems like an eternity, she reaches the end of the hallway. The children and the man with the compelling voice are gone. The young woman looks in all directions but there is no one there. She looks above and realizes she is standing outside and there is nothing but dark grey clouds. Rain pours down and the young woman's dress is drenched and clinging to her extremely thin frame. It's all so forceful, so real.

Lea was jolted awake by the sound of a howling wind. She wondered what time it was. She leaned over to see if her new roommate was awake. She might know the time. Unfortunately for Lea, the woman was sound asleep. Not able to go back there herself, Lea lay still on the bed and stared out the window. The sky was pitch black. Certainly, it was hours yet before daybreak.

Lea hated to wake up in the middle of the night. Many times, she would be stirred awake from awful, vivid nightmares. Once in a while, she would have wonderful dreams, where would be holding her baby in her arms, or coddling her toddler, or in the arms of her loving husband. But then, she would be taken away or prevented from being with them. Most of the time, her dreams ended in anguish.

Lea stared at the ceiling. Her heart was beating fast, as though she truly had been trying to walk through a windstorm. Her hospital nightgown was damp, likely from the fever. She took a deep breath and tried to calm herself down. It was only a dream, she thought. It is just the sound of the wind.

She thought about her last visit with Louis, and revelled at the chance that he might bring Jean with him this coming Sunday. She delighted in the thought of possibly seeing her son in less than two days. She hoped and prayed to God that the weather would cooperate.

Unfortunately, by the time Sunday arrived, the young boy had a mild fever and Louis ended up visiting Lea on his own. He could not possibly take the child out on a horse buggy in the dead of winter. Also, the more Louis thought about it, the more he felt uneasy about bringing Jean to a building full of sick people. Likewise, he did not want to expose Lea to whatever it was that Jean had. He shuddered at the thought of having to bear more illness in his family.

Louis immediately saw the look of frustration on his wife's face and tried to thwart this with a loving embrace. He then explained why young Jean had to stay at home, and promised that he would bring him as soon as the child felt better. Seeing that Lea was still disappointed, Louis lay down beside his wife, careful not to touch her wounds, and said, "Close your eyes, Lea. Put your arm around me and let's just pretend we're at home on our sofa." And that they did. For most of this visit they lay side by side, barely saying a word, cherishing their time together.

Before leaving, Louis picked up the bag of goodies he had brought over from her mother and sisters. The bag was filled with a Christmas garland made of pinecones and ribbons from one sister, a bottle of homemade wine from another, some homemade bread from Mme. Michaud and two jars of jelly from Lea's mother. Louis watched Lea as she took each item out of the bag and smiled. What he knew for sure, though, was that as grateful as she was to receive these items from her family, nothing could compare to the smile she would have had on her face if he had walked in the door with little Jean.

December 15, 1932

Chère Maman,

I received your letter yesterday. Thank you so much for sending me a dollar. Louis also gave me the two packages of jam. They are very good. Since I've been here, they have only given me honey on toast in between meals... now I am able to have some of your wonderful jelly!

Being sick is difficult. I have no doubt that you are doing everything you can for the little ones, but this has added so much work and disruption to your life. I am sure you must often be tired. You tell me not to worry and be upset about the children, but how can I not be! It has been nine weeks since I've been here and I have no idea when I can even get out of bed. There are many days when I am very discouraged.

I was so happy to write to Louis yesterday, to tell him that the leaking from my wounds had stopped, but today, the leaking is worse than ever, plus my stomach is completely bloated. This is bothering me so much! The doctor came to see me yesterday but did not say a word.

M. Gauvreau wrote his wife to tell her that he was sure you could take a train to and from Grande Clairière in one day.

Pass my letter on to Louis. I will write him on Wednesday. That is all for today. I hope that I can give you some better news one day. I am sure that I will be here for a while yet.

Kisses to Jean and Maurice… and to you too. Your daughter who loves you, Lea

Lea felt so indebted to her mother. Not only was she the boys' main caregiver, she also found ways to take care of Lea. Everything she sent to Lea at the hospital was sent with such thoughtfulness. The jars of strawberry and apple jelly were delicious and allowed Lea a bit of variety, instead of the same, monotonous food day after day. The money Lea received from Maman would go a long way. One dollar, combined with the dollar she had when she first arrived, could buy her some needed items not provided by the hospital, or perhaps gifts for the boys for Christmas.

The possibility of having a visit from her eldest son was never far from Lea's thoughts. As it was, she hadn't seen him in over two months. Ever since Louis had suggested that he and her mother might bring Jean to the hospital, Lea could not erase it from her mind. She had been so sure she would see him the previous Sunday, but it was not to be. Now, another week gone by, the probability seemed to be withering away. The hope of seeing Jean, followed by two weeks of not seeing him, had Lea in agony.

The original idea was for them to come to Souris by horse and sleigh, or ask someone in town with an automobile to drive them up. The weather was wreaking havoc with any plans, and as the winter progressed, chances were getting slimmer by the day.

The one glimmer of hope that Lea had was that her mother could take Jean by train. According to Mme. Gauvreau's husband, she could do this in one day and be back in Grande Clairière before supper. Lea hoped and prayed that this could happen.

She needed to see Jean, if only for a short time. More than anything, she needed to see, feel, and hold her own flesh and blood. Nothing else mattered.

December 20, 1932
Cher Louis,

It's always pretty much the same here. I'm not in pain but one of the sores is leaking. I was so happy when I was able to write you that it hadn't leaked for two days. I thought then that I was on my way to healing, but it looks as though I have more to go through for the moment. The doctor tells me things are looking better than they were, but it is taking such a long time. He also told me yesterday that Madame Pallard called to find out how I was. Is it you that made her call?

I'm sure you find the time as long as I do. But let's be brave. Perhaps we still have a chance to be happy. Every night, I dream that I am back home, and believe me when I say that I am so happy in these dreams to be back with you, and Jean and Maurice. But then I wake up each morning and I see myself here. I'm done. I will write you again in the next day or so.

Hug Jean and Maurice often for me.
Kisses to you from afar,
Lea

Each time Louis retrieved the mail from the post office, Mme. Pallard would ask him how Lea was doing. Most times, he gave her a quick update, and most times he wasn't bothered at all by her asking. Lately though, he was finding it difficult to know what to say.

Lea was not in a horrible state, but she wasn't improving either. The doctors were not really revealing what exactly was happening and it was difficult to understand why she wasn't healing. Lea's letters were getting repetitive, so much so that Louis could barely get through reading them. It upset him to know that his wife was still in distress and disturbed him even more to know that she was getting discouraged. Lea. Discouraged. She usually had such a positive outlook on life. If she was finding the situation hopeless, then it certainly must be.

So the last time Louis had gone into the store, when Mme. Pallard asked him about his wife's condition, he sternly suggested she had the luxury of a telephone and could therefore call the hospital and find out for herself. He later regretted being so gruff with his friendly and caring neighbour, but his nerves were starting to fray.

Back home, lying on the sofa alone, Louis looked over the last letter from Lea. He reread the last paragraph and let out a sigh. What completely escaped him was the fact that Christmas was just a few days away and it had not even crossed his mind that he should buy a little something for his wife and sons. When he did think about it, he knew he didn't have any extra money to buy anything.

Louis knew how important it was for Lea to see Jean. Seeing him would be the best Christmas present she could ever receive. The Sunday before Christmas came and went. It was much too cold to attempt a horse ride to Souris, twenty degrees below zero. Fortunately, temperatures warmed up slightly a few days later, just enough to make travelling bearable.

Still below zero, but with no wind and sunny skies, Louis, Sylvie and little Jean headed out to Souris in his brother's horse-drawn sleigh. Sylvie made certain that they took along two hand-knitted blankets to cover their heads and shoulders. They also wore old lap robes made of buffalo hides to cover their thighs, legs and feet. Little Jean sat between Louis and Sylvie, and the warmth of their bodies helped to keep the child from getting too cold.

The sky was azure blue and the sun shone brightly, which was a blessing. The trek to Souris would take at least two hours by horse. Sylvie quietly hoped that the sun would continue to shine all day long so that their return ride would be just as comfortable. For now, she could see that she had nothing to worry about; not a cloud could be seen across the entire spectrum of the expansive prairie sky.

On the way down, Sylvie explained to Jean that he would only be able to see his mother for a short while. She told him gently that Maman was very sick and weak and would not be able to hold him. To console him, she told him that with any luck at all, and by the grace of God, he would have his mother home soon. For a two and a half year old, all that mattered was that he was on a special sleigh ride to see his Maman, whom he hadn't seen for a very long time. He smiled in anticipation. On either side of the sleigh, mounds of snow lay on miles of flat land. The lull of the landscape made the ride pleasant.

By the time they arrived in Souris, some two hours later, the toddler had fallen asleep on his grandmother's lap. Sylvie jostled him so that he would wake up. Reluctantly, Jean opened his eyes and saw the large brick building before him. He stepped onto the frozen ground, and began to walk toward the hospital doors, still holding his grandmother's hand.

As they stepped inside the hospital, they were greeted by Nurse Edna. She knew full well that Jean was coming for a visit—Lea had been talking about this for some time now—and she had prepared the main floor waiting room so that Lea could be carried down from the second floor and wheeled in on the hospital's newly-acquired gatch bed. Though it was not hospital policy to let children visit patients at the hospital, an exception was made in the case of Lea Mahy. Dr. Fraser, at the urging of Nurse Edna, had approved the visit, as long as it was limited to under an hour and on the condition that the patient did not attempt to carry the child. Lea reluctantly agreed to both conditions. She had wished that she could hold and coddle her oldest boy—both her babies for that matter—for hours on end. Reality sunk in however and she knew that any pulling on her badly-scarred wounds could cause severe problems, which would make it even longer before she could go home to them.

Jean was still groggy and appeared shy when he saw Nurse Edna. When he saw the tall, auburn-haired woman dressed in a long white dress, a short black cape and a cap on her head, he hid behind his grandmother and peered out, only to see a huge rolling bed coming toward him. He had never seen such a contraption. He began to whimper, but stopped immediately when he saw what appeared to be his mother.

Lea gave her mother a huge grin. She was so happy to see her after all this time, and wanted nothing more than the ability to leap from her bed and give her dear maman a great big hug. But first, more than anything, she wanted to hold her little boy in her loving arms.

"Jean, mon cher petit. Vient-voir maman."

He immediately recognized her voice. Lying in bed, Lea leaned over to the side of the rail and reached out her arms as best she could. Jean slowly approached the bed and stood beside her, barely nose-high to the mattress. Sylvie lifted the child just enough so that he could sit on the edge of the bed. The young mother and her son glared into each other's eyes. Jean smiled wryly. Lea's eyes welled up with tears.

The visit was subdued and went by quickly. Most of Lea's questions to her son were answered with a bashful nod.

"Are you being a good boy for Grandmaman?" The young boy nodded shyly.

"Are you helping her by looking after your little brother?" Nod.

"Do you like staying at Grandmaman's house?" Nod.

Jean stayed equally close to both his mother and his more recent caregiver, Grandmaman Charles. Grandmaman was his security now. He didn't quite recognize the woman in the strange bed with wheels. Though she sounded like Maman, this woman looked different. She was pale and weak.

During the entire visit, Louis stood at the entrance of the waiting room. He watched closely as Lea absorbed the moment of seeing her son after such a long separation. He observed little Jean, apprehensive yet loving, interact with his mother. Louis recognized the undeniable bond between his wife and son. He remained at the door for the entire visit, just seeing the visit unfold and doing his utmost to hold back tears.

Just as Jean was becoming familiar with his surroundings, he was told they had to leave. He let the frail woman in the bed kiss him on the forehead and then on both cheeks. He began to cry, unable to comprehend why, after finding his mother, he would be taken away from her again. Grandmaman took him in her arms and reassured him that everything would be alright. He wasn't upset for long. After all, Grandmaman had said his "real" mother would be coming home soon. He believed that, just as he believed that the Père Noel would soon be coming to visit Grande Clairière. Sylvie kissed her daughter goodbye and led the young boy out of the room.

The ride back home was incredibly long and cold. Though it was barely late afternoon, the sun was beginning to fade. After all, it was one day before the winter solstice. The kaleidoscopic variations of pink scattered across the southwestern sky were a distraction for a short while, but not enough to last the entire ride home. Jean no longer saw the ride as a novelty and was boisterous to say the least. Louis had to raise his voice for the young boy to settle down. As Sylvie sat shivering in the sleigh with Jean in her arms, she could only think about how her daughter looked on this day that should have been so special. Sylvie found Lea to be gaunt and frail, and even though Lea smiled throughout the entire visit, Sylvie could see an underlying sadness sweeping over her.

That evening, Lea spoke to Nurse Edna about what had transpired earlier in the day.

"If I am hospitalized much longer, my sons may not recognize me at all."

"Lea, you can't worry about that."

Lea went on to other thoughts that clouded her mind.

"Why did the hospital limit the time I could spend with Jean?"

Though she was thankful that Jean was able to sit on her bed, she wished so much that she could have sat up and held him.

"I so wish that I could have held him in my arms, Edna. I just wanted to pamper him and shower him with a thousand kisses. I just wanted to hold him."

For two months now, Lea had been asking her husband and family to embrace her two boys via her letters. Now she had the opportunity to do so herself, yet when the time came, she could barely sit up. Frustration set in as she wondered how much more of this she could endure before she began to fall apart. Here it was, just a few days before Christmas, a time of year she loved so very much. She had so hoped she could be home by this time. She longed to be with Louis, preparing for this sacred time. She wanted to be with her little ones, to tell them about bébé Jésus and give them each a gift chosen just for them. She wished that she was well enough to gather with family and friends at church for midnight mass, especially to listen to M. Bauche sing "Minuit Chrétien." She thought of past Christmases and the great times shared with family following mass for the traditional réveillon. Everyone would gather at Maman's to feast on appetizers and a grand meal that included roast pork, mashed potatoes and gravy. The children especially loved all the Christmas baking and the adults indulged in fortified wine until about four in the morning. Good times were always had on this special occasion. She eventually calmed down and reminded herself that a new year was just around the corner. Perhaps 1933 would be a better year for her and her family.

December 29, 1932
Cher Louis,

A word to wish you a Happy New Year and especially, to wish you good health. I thought you might come to visit me yesterday, because you told me you would come sometime this week. I know this will upset you, but I suffered greatly yesterday, when the doctor made the wound that is leaking bigger to put two tubes in. I assure you, this is not encouraging. I was much stronger just a few days ago, and now, here I am again. I am only eating soup three times a day—no bread, no nothing. I often wonder if I will ever recover from this. I think of my two dear ones all the time. You should see how much blood I have on me. The doctor hasn't been here yet today, and when he does come, he will probably cause me pain again. I think I should stop writing for today. You have enough sadness to absorb in one letter. Kisses to you, and don't forget the little ones.

Lea

Christmas had come and gone, and Louis was thankful for the days he was able to spend at home in Grande Clairière. The lack of railroad work during the Christmas season was a blessing in disguise. It gave Louis the opportunity to help Sylvie tend to a few household chores—filling the wood box, cutting ice for the ice box, and repairing the door to the outhouse. More importantly, he was able to spend much of his spare time with his children. Both boys seemed to be adapting well to their new surroundings and were quite well-behaved for his mother-in-law. He was pleased that he didn't have to deal with disobedient children on top of everything else.

Louis also took the time to visit with family and friends. He took Jean by horse and buggy a few times to visit Grandmère Mahy and some of his aunts and uncles in the area. Young Jean enjoyed the special attention he received when he spent time alone with his father. Moreover, he loved winter sleigh rides.

Just after Christmas, Louis spent a day in Virden with some of his train buddies. In the early morning, he boarded the CNR train that ran through Grande Clairière and headed up through Belleview and Scarth to the town of Virden. He met up with friends and they spent the day frequenting a few stores down Nelson Street and Seventh Avenue. He found a good sale at the local jewellery store and purchased a new watch for Lea, a belated Christmas present. The group of buddies then went to the Victoria Billiard Hall and ended their day at the beer parlour at the Alexandra Hotel. Louis hopped on the last freight train out of Virden and arrived in Grande Clairière in the early morning hours.

Louis visited Lea four times over the course of ten days, which was much more than he had ever been able to do since she'd been in Souris. He drove up with Father Bertrand once, and went another time by horse and sleigh with Léon and Palmyre. He also went up by train one day with Pierre and Nora Hardy. Visitors seemed to make the time pass a little faster for Lea and she always had a huge smile for all her visitors, but especially Louis, every time he showed up at her bedside. All in all, Louis was happy with the way he was able to spend the last two weeks.

But after reading Lea's letter, Louis felt unbearable sorrow, more than he'd ever allowed himself to feel before. For the first time since Lea was admitted to hospital, he confronted the fact that she may never heal from this dreadful operation. The infection seemed to have a stranglehold on her. For a moment, he imagined life without her, but then quickly caught himself. No, he could not think that. This would not, *could not*, happen.

The railway had been in touch with Louis by telegram and he was scheduled to return to work in early January. Just prior to heading out to Minto, where parts of the railroad line needed new ties, he knew he had to make his way to Souris one more time. His wife needed him at her side. He needed to see her and give her words of encouragement. They both needed to hope that this year would bring better days.

December 29, 1932
Chère Maman,

I would have never believed when I left you earlier this year that I would now be sending you wishes for a Happy New Year on a piece of paper. It is with all my heart that I wish you a happy and especially healthy new year. I received the slippers and I thank you very much. They put them under the Christmas tree here and the women from Souris also gave me a big box of biscuits, an orange chocolate cake and two canning jars of jelly.

You will see from the letter I wrote to Louis that things aren't going so well. I would somehow be so proud if I could just put my feet on the ground. I often wonder if I will ever heal. It's infuriating that it is winter, because otherwise you could come and see me. I know that this would be impossible for you to do with little Maurice. Don't tire yourself out too much. Get help if you can. I'm sure Bertha is ready to help you, as she always has been. I will stop writing now as I am tired. No one will ever know what I have suffered. It is horrible to be in this situation. Happy New Year to all my brothers and sisters.

Your daughter who thinks of you often,
Lea

As Sylvie carried a large crate of Christmas decorations from inside the house to the shed, she felt a slight tightness in her chest from carrying the heavy box. She stopped to catch her breath, but the crisp winter air ate away at her exposed skin, so she decided to trudge along, regardless of the pain. She opened the rickety door to the shed, stored the box away in a corner, and hurried back to the house.

Christmas this year had been so different than past years. Sylvie had decided against lighting as many candles this year, concerned that Jean and Maurice would touch them. Instead, she crafted some garland made of corn husks and dried fruit to decorate her home.

She spent some time knitting mitts and slippers for Lea's boys and purchased some candy canes from Pallard's store to add to the brown paper wrapping on their gifts. She also knit a pair of slippers for each of her own children, including Lea, a gift she sent with Louis to Souris Hospital on Christmas Day. She would have liked to have sent her daughter a photograph of the little boys, but she hadn't found the time to send the film to Winnipeg for developing. Life was just too busy.

There were no huge festivities at Sylvie Charles' house on Christmas day. Sylvie and Louis had originally thought to bring the boys to the hospital so that Lea could see her sons on this sacred occasion. Father Bertrand had even offered to take the family to the hospital in his Essex once the Christmas morning mass was over. This wasn't to be however, as the temperature dipped once again. It was just too dangerous to drive such a long way with young children. Instead, Louis and the priest went alone for the day. They brought Lea a few gifts from various family members and a large piece of Maman's three-tiered fruitcake.

Sylvie invited Louis' mother over to spend the day with her and their grandchildren. Sylvie's son Emile came by and took them all on a sleigh ride into town to see la Crèche inside the front of the church. This was a beautiful manger, hand-crafted and set up each year by parishioners on Christmas Eve. Many people from far away towns would come by to see the lavish display. Later that evening, Sylvie, Louis, his mother, Léon, Palmyre, little Aurélie, Jean, and baby Maurice, gathered around the table to share in a delicious, but somewhat low-key Christmas dinner. Sylvie cooked a small chicken, roasted some potatoes, and opened a jar of beans that Lea had canned in the early fall. Just before eating, they lit a special Christmas candle and gave thanks to the Lord for all of their blessings.

After all, they were blessed that Lea was still alive and had so far made it through some difficult times. Sylvie was thankful that she was receiving a lot of help lately. Most of her daughters and a few of her granddaughters took turns taking care of Jean and Maurice, and this indeed was a blessing.

Palmyre had been ever so supportive since she'd moved back to Grande Clairière, even though she wasn't feeling all that well herself. Sylvie predicted that her youngest daughter was probably expecting another child, and she was right. A test at a local nursing station a few days later confirmed that she was to have a baby in April or May of 1933. This would be the forty-second grandchild for Sylvie.

The New Year also came in without any fanfare. No party at the Charles' house this year. No dancing. No music. No table spread with cooking and baking, except for the three-tiered fruitcake and a bûche de Noël. Many of her children and grandchildren visited sporadically throughout the day, but were treated only to a few sweet delicacies and coffee or tea, and soda pop for the children.

The lack of merriment and celebration actually worked in Sylvie's favour. Without all the preparations for her annual fête, she took some time to rest. Sylvie knew that she needed to get her energy level back up if she was to look after the boys for much longer. Lea was showing no significant signs of improvement, so Sylvie set her mind that she might be taking care of her young grandsons for quite a while.

CHAPTER 5

January 1933

January 4, 1933
Ma chère Lea,

I wish you a much better year than last year. I hope to go see you next week, time and weather permitting. Do you think I should bring little Maurice, or is it better to leave him at home? What do you think? This New Year was much sadder for us than last year. We miss you and hope that you won't be there much longer. For now, all we can do is be strong. Alice often comes over to help me. I've already told her that she has enough to do with her own family and shouldn't worry about us, but she still comes by.

See you next week,
Your mother, Sylvie Charles

After reading her mother's letter, Lea felt her heart beat faster and she let out a huge smile. Just the thought of seeing her baby again was enough to make her tingle with happiness. She was still holding onto the memory of seeing Jean in December. Now she needed another one of those moments with her youngest son. She longed to feel the tenderness of the only two little people in this world that belonged to her.

Then again, she knew that the unpredictable prairie winter could have a say in whether her mother could attempt the visit. Lea inquired about the running of the trains from Grande Clairière to Souris. The nurses knew for sure that it was possible to take a train around lunch time in Hartney and another train returned from Souris to Hartney at four p.m. That would give her mother at least three hours to go to the hospital and get to and from the train station. That would give them at least two hours to visit with each other; the train station was a fair distance away from the hospital. Lea immediately realized that somehow, they would have to arrange for a ride. Her mother could not possibly walk all that way, in the cold, with baby Maurice in her arms. Nevertheless, Lea hoped and prayed that this plan would somehow work out and she would see her baby boy once again.

Lea was so grateful to her family for helping her mother, even though they all had enough turmoil in their own lives. Her sister Alice had seven children, three of them under the ages of five, and the youngest a mere baby, born just a few weeks before Lea had been hospitalized. In fact, Lea had helped to look after Alice's older children when the baby was born. Lea recently found out that Alice's husband hadn't been feeling well lately. Lea's heart warmed at the thought of her sister putting aside her own troubles to help out her extended family.

But she was guilt-stricken as she realized how busy everyone was, partially because of her, and all she ever did was lay flat on her hospital bed, alone and with nothing to do. Times were even lonelier for Lea, as Mme. Gauvreau had been released from the hospital just before Christmas. The sweet old woman promised to visit Lea as soon as she was well enough to travel from Hartney to Souris. Lea expected this would not be possible for quite a while.

Nurse Edna walked in the room, felt Lea's forehead and reached for a thermometer. "You look downhearted this evening."

"My family has been incredible through this ordeal. I don't know how I will ever thank them."

"You'll find a way. Right now, it's more important that you rest. It helps, Lea. Your health is improving with all the rest you've been getting."

Lea didn't see it. If she was getting better, why wasn't she being sent back home? Three months, Lea repeated to herself. Three months since I've been here. Certainly she would be out before the snow melted. She decided she would aim for this. Early March would be a wonderful time to go back to Grande Clairière. What she wanted more than anything was to go home, to be with her husband and her children, and to settle back in her normal life, surrounded by friends and family.

January 6, 1933
Chère Maman,

I received your letter yesterday and am very happy to hear that you will be coming to visit me next week. As for bringing Maurice, I would be very happy to see him, but if you have someone to stay home with him, I believe that might be easier for you. The train station is a long way from the hospital. You would have to get a ride from someone in Souris. As it is, the baby is so heavy to carry.

As for me, it is always the same thing… the wounds are leaking all the time. Lately, they have been washing my wound with a strong liquid that looks like water, and let me tell you, it hurts. Does Jean still talk about me? Maurice—he will only know his grandmother. I have nothing left to say. Please pass my letter on to Louis.

Your daughter who thinks of you,

Lea

On a dark, cloudy morning in early January, Nurse Edna walked into Lea's room to examine her patient. Lea lay sleeping, even though it was mid-morning. The darkness of the room likely helped to make her patient doze off. Edna pulled the blanket back and raised the hospital gown slightly to expose Lea's abdomen. Her stomach was still distended and the sores were clearly infected. On this particular morning, the plan was to drain and dress her wound once again. The nurse trusted that this procedure would not be as painful for Lea as the last one had been.

As Edna placed her hand on her patient's forehead, Lea slowly opened her eyes. She smiled faintly and said "I might see my baby this week. My mother is considering taking the train here with Maurice."

"Well, that will be quite the treat" the nurse looked at Lea and smiled. "Let's see if we can improve your comfort in the meantime."

"She will need help with transportation" Lea continued. "She can't carry my baby from the train station to the hospital. It's just too far."

"I'll see what I can do" Nurse Edna reassured her. "I have a brother who may be able to help. For now, try to relax."

Nurse Edna proceeded to wash her patient's wounds with a saline solution. The last time she did this was with peroxide, and she couldn't bear to hear Lea scream in pain. Saline would be a little more bearable.

Concerned with the swelling of her abdomen, nurse Edna also took the time to place cloths drenched in hot water on Lea's stomach, hoping this would alleviate the inflammation.

As she headed back to the nurse's quarters after her shift, the young nurse thought how important it was to arrange a car ride for Lea's mother. Edna wondered how she herself would handle not being able to see her sons for such a long period of time. As it was, she had to work for a living, and being away from them for ten to twelve hour periods at a time was sometimes agonizing. But such was the life of a widow. She wondered if telling Lea her story would help her young patient cope. Somehow, hearing someone else's troubles sometimes soothes the pain of your own.

January 10, 1933
Cher Louis,

A few lines to give you a bit of my news, as I am sure you are always happy to receive one of my letters. Not much to tell you… things are always the same. Now they are putting cloths drenched in hot water on my stomach to make the swelling go down. I'm not sure that this is doing any good. The leaking continues. Please tell my mother to bring my white watch when she comes. Do you know which one I mean?

Unfortunately, the one you bought me doesn't work well. You will have to remove the elastic bracelet and replace it with the black ribbon. The watch is on the dresser and the ribbon is in the glass bowl. That's all for today. Kiss Jean and Maurice for me. I love you with all my heart.

Lea Mahy

On the same day Louis received this letter, he retrieved Lea's watch from the dresser, and trekked over to Sylvie's house, so she could bring it to Lea. Today was the day she had planned to take a train ride to Souris with the baby. Three miles was a long way to walk in the bitter cold, but Louis thought it was important that he deliver this to Sylvie before he headed out to work.

He arrived at Sylvie's house well before she was about to leave. As he stepped through the front door, he could see that she was already preparing a bag to take on her journey—some food items, diapers and a change of clothes for baby Maurice.

"Lea asked for this watch," he told Sylvie. "The one I bought her is apparently not working."

He also handed her a bottle of dandelion wine. He had heard that this particular wine was full of healing powers, and he wanted Lea to give it a try. Then, he headed back toward town so he could prepare to go to work.

Sylvie added the two items to the bag. Family members had also gathered some items to lift Lea's spirits—a knitted shawl, a pair of wool socks, and a hand-sewn nightgown, so that Lea could wear something other than that dreadful hospital attire.

Though the baby was oblivious to what the day would bring, Sylvie could not help but be overjoyed that her grandson would once again be with his mother. She had received a telegram from Edna at Souris Hospital that transportation had been arranged for her once she arrived in Souris. She was grateful to Lea's kind nurse for arranging this.

Lea's sister Bertha tended to Jean for the day. The toddler had grown quite accustomed to being with any one of his many relatives by now and made no fuss.

Sylvie had arranged for her son Georges to take her and the baby to Pallard's store by sleigh. Only one train ran from Grande Clairière to Hartney on weekdays, at 10:20 a.m. She arrived at the general store well before the train was scheduled to arrive, giving her ample time to visit with the storekeeper and his wife.

Upon seeing Sylvie, Mme. Pallard took a jar of strawberry preserve off the shelf. "Give this to Lea from us," she said. Sylvie thanked the storekeeper's wife for her thoughtfulness. She added it to the bag of items.

When the time came, M. Pallard took the train passengers—Sylvie, the baby, and three other travellers—in his truck, and they headed a half mile up the road to the passenger shelter. Thankfully, on this cold winter day, the storeowner had taken the time to fill the shelter's coal stove. Sylvie sat comfortably on the wooden bench and held her grandchild in her arms until the CN passenger train arrived. The sound of the steam locomotive could be heard well before the train pulled up at the station.

As Sylvie settled into the red leather seat on the train, warmed up partly from the sun and partly from the coal stove situated at the back of the car, she looked out the window and couldn't help but notice the expansive clearing in front of her. On this bright day, she could see for miles. The frigid air had caused floating ice crystals in the air, adding to the beauty of the scenery. She enjoyed the view, even as the train sped off, and marvelled at the splendour of the Manitoba prairies on this cold, winter day. Looking across the aisle to the windows facing south, she could see the sand hills in the distance. Before she knew it, she was in Hartney, where she prepared for the next leg of her journey.

The train from Hartney to Souris—no. 138—was scheduled to leave at 12:28 p.m. She had to walk over to the CP station, three blocks away, but she had plenty of time to do so. In fact, it gave her enough time to visit Hartney's well-known general store on East Railway Street. She went there so rarely, especially since the depression had set in, and since she had been looking after her grandsons.

Hill's General Store sold everything from groceries to dry goods to clothing. Sylvie headed to the ladies' goods department and looked through some of the

beautiful clothing and hats. It was all too expensive. She
headed over to the more affordable items and looked
through the various lines of cosmetics. She found a light
raspberry-toned lipstick and immediately thought of
Lea. "This might bring a bit of colour to her colourless
complexion," thought Sylvie, and decided to purchase it
for her. She added the small gift to the bag of goodies.

By the time she left the store, enough time had passed
that she had to walk rather briskly to the CP station down
the street. By the time she boarded the second train,
Maurice was restless and hungry. Sylvie settled into her
seat and immediately fed the baby a small canning jar of
fruit, followed by a bottle of milk.

The train ride from Hartney to Souris took approxi-
mately thirty minutes. When the train arrived at the
grand masonry station in Souris, Sylvie gathered her
things and lifted her grandson, who by now had fallen
asleep on the seat beside her, and headed to the exit. She
stepped onto the platform, felt the brisk and biting air,
and quickly made her way through to the interior of the
station. There, she waited momentarily until a tall, kind-
looking gentleman approached her, telling her he was
Nurse Edna's brother and that he would be driving her
to the hospital. Sylvie thanked him and gladly handed
him fifty cents for his troubles. As they stepped outside
and walked to the car, the chill in the air rustled baby
Maurice up momentarily and he began to cry. When
they settled into the fairly new covered vehicle, the baby

soon leaned his head back down on Grandmaman's shoulder and fell asleep.

Once they arrived at the hospital, the gentleman helped Sylvie carry Maurice up the steps, to the hospital's front door. They were immediately greeted by a nurse, who took them directly to Lea's room. When they arrived, Lea was sitting up, slightly. When she saw her child in the tall man's arms, she immediately cradled her arms to the side, and asked him to place the baby in her arms. Nurse Edna nodded in approval and placed a pillow to support the child. Sylvie stationed herself close by, in case she needed to pick Maurice up, and watch intently as her ailing daughter interacted with her young son.

Lea marveled at this big, beautiful baby in her arms. It was incredulous to her that this was Maurice. He had grown so much and his features seemed so different than the last time she had seen him. She spent a good five minutes in silence, just staring down at this angelic child, stroking his forehead and the sides of his cheeks, all the while smiling from ear to ear.

"Quel beau, gros bébé!" she whispered.

When Maurice awoke, Sylvie held him, but kept him as close to her daughter as possible. Most times, Maurice woke up happy, and this day was no different. He smiled at Lea and babbled and cooed, all to the young mother's delight. There were a few times however, where the baby

only wanted to be held by his grandmother. Lea sadly
acccptcd this and did not let it upset her. She reminded
herself that there was some comfort in knowing that
Maurice was so attached to his grandmother.

The two-hour visit went by much too quickly for Lea.
She and her mother shared stories and kept the conversation pleasant and low-key. Lea looked at the many items
in the bag filled with presents—the jar of preserve from
Mme. Pallard, the clothing items from her sisters, the
lipstick from her mother, her white watch and the bottle
of wine from Louis. How thoughtful, she thought, that
Louis had sent her watch so quickly. She had told him
about waking up from dreams in the middle of the night
and not knowing the time. He must have taken that to
heart. She thanked her mother for bringing all these
items along and asked her to thank everyone for their
overwhelming generosity. How she wished she could
thank them herself... thank Louis herself... hold him in
her arms, just as she was holding her youngest child at
this very moment.

During this visit, Lea spent as much time as she
could tending to her young son. She cradled him in her
arms when he let her, caressing his soft skin, adoring
his beautiful face. This was one of the best days Lea had
spent since she had been hospitalized. After her sorrowful visit with Jean, when she was made painfully aware
that she wasn't able to care for him, and he barely knew
her, she expected this visit to be more of the same. She

was pleasantly surprised that she was able to maneuver herself enough to hold her baby during the visit. She hoped for many more days like this. She prayed that she would be home soon, to hold and caress her baby boys and her loving husband. Surely, to God, she and her family had experienced enough tragedy.

January 16, 1933
Dear Louis,

I received the wine. I have some three times a day. I have suffered quite a bit since my mother's visit. Last Thursday. I had some x-rays taken, as they were afraid I might have tuberculosis. After they were taken however, they told me there were no spots anywhere and no sign of the disease. On Friday, they cut my abscess open just above the fold of my leg. They cut me without putting me to sleep. You can just imagine how much I screamed. So now I have two wounds that are leaking and not just a little…they are changing my bandages at least ten times a day, and each time they do, the bed is soaked in blood. I'm not telling you this to make you feel bad, but I think you should know. Maybe things will improve today.

I asked for a raw egg this morning for break-fast, but they did not give me one. They said I

*might get one later in the morning, but I think
I will have to buy my own eggs if I want some.*

*If mother had not been with Maurice last
week, I don't think I would have recognized
him. He is so big!*

*That is all for today. Give kisses and hugs to
my two dear little ones. When will I have the
pleasure of seeing them again? They bring me
such joy!*

Love, Lea

Reading about how Lea barely recognized her own
baby, Louis could not help but think that, over the last
two months, Lea had become barely recognizable herself.
She had lost so much weight. Her cheeks were sunken,
she was ashen and she no longer had that glow about
her. She was so extremely tiny and her voice was so soft
that, at times, she looked and sounded like a child. He
thought back to those early days, when he had first met
Lea in Grande Clairière.

Louis Mahy was in his early teens when he moved
to Canada. At that time, Lea was only six years old. He
knew who she was growing up, but never really paid
much attention to her. While working as a farmhand, he
became friends with a few of Lea's older brothers. Still,
Lea was merely just someone he knew. The summer following his family's arrival in Grande Clairière, the town
held a twenty-fifth anniversary celebration of St. Jean

parish. Louis vaguely remembered her running a sack race at the church picnic, where she was teamed up with her sister Palmyre. The two of them were well ahead of all the other teams and won first prize, a bag full of candy. When they won, the young girls fell to the ground, both still in the burlap sack that rose up above their waists, and rolled around in the grass giggling and squealing in delight. Both Louis and his brother Léon noticed them and commented on their giddiness, but both were struck by their "joie de vivre." Ironically, years later, the two boys married those same two women.

In fact, fifteen years after Louis had first laid eyes on Lea, he began to see her in a different light. A taller, slender Lea, now a maturing young woman, caught his attention at a town dance. She had silky black hair and large, piercing blue eyes. Once he got to know her better, he realized that she could read and write quite well. She was intelligent and level-headed... not at all frivolous or mischievous like so many other girls. Moreover, she was strong-willed and even a little feisty at times. In her early twenties, Lea was still unmarried, uncommon for that time. This boded well for Louis, as he himself was still a bachelor heading into his thirties.

They saw each other at church and social gatherings, and out and about town, and spent some time just flirting with each other, but nothing came of it. Then, his brother and her sister fell in love, and now, suddenly, Louis was invited to all the Charles' family parties. By the time Léon and Palmyre were married in February 1927, Louis and Lea realized that they were completely smitten with each other. They dated for a little over a year, and then began to seriously plan their life together.

Louis and Lea were married in St. Jean's Catholic Church in Grande Clairière on a balmy November day in 1928. They had a rousing wedding reception at Maman's house. Though the house was a few miles away from the church, many guests took to walking there, as the weather was above freezing, quite unusual for the month of November. Most of their family members were in attendance, even a few relatives from as far away as Saskatchewan. Lea was particularly happy that her sister Palmyre was able to attend, even though she had just given birth to little Aurélie a few months earlier. November was often an impossible month to travel in Manitoba, especially with a young baby, but this particular year, the late fall weather was unusually mild. Though the town of Bernice was not that far from Grande Clairière, the roads to and from there were not gravelled or graded, so any amounts of snow on the ground could have impeded their chance at getting to the wedding. Lea and Palmyre were extremely close. The fact that they married brothers made them even closer.

Louis was anxious to get back to Souris, to see his wife, yes, but also to talk to Dr. Fraser. Lea's letter mentioned she had been tested for tuberculosis, and that had Louis extremely worried. That possibility had never been mentioned to him before. All along, the thought was that Lea was suffering from a severe infection caused by delayed wound healing from the operation. Never before had tuberculosis been brought up. That dreaded illness had already caused enough havoc with Louis' family. He wanted to ask the doctor what led them to think she might have it in the first place. And, even though the tests had come back negative, did the possibility that she may have it still exist?

Louis was concerned with Lea's progress, or lack of it. He had come across some literature that proposed drinking fortified wine daily would help cure infections, just as he had heard that swallowing raw eggs might help. He was grasping at straws, trying to find his own solutions to healing his wife. The medical system had failed him before. He could not bear to have it fail him again.

January 22, 1933
Dear Louis,

I received your letter yesterday. I'm doing well enough, but as always, my wounds are leaking. I spent a few days not eating, but am now eating well. You tell me to be more demanding. This is easier said than done. I have meat to eat but once a week. I've asked for more than this, but they told me that they could not

*give patients meat more than once a week,
as that would be too costly for the hospital. I
asked the doctor if I could have some however,
and he said he would arrange something. So
last Saturday, the nurse brought me five huge
pieces of roast beef for ten cents.*

*You tell me that you had the flu. You must take
care of yourself. I found you to be very thin the
last time you were here. I hope that the boys
are well. Little Maurice sure is attached to
my mother.*

*When will we be together as a family again? If
it wasn't for this latest setback, I would probably be healing much faster, but this abscess
has become wicked.*

*Please let your mother know how I am doing,
as I don't have much energy to write. My
stomach is big, as always.*

*Kisses to Jean Maurice…
and of course to you as well.
Lea*

The year 1933 started bleakly. Economically, Canada
was still feeling the effects of the 1929 stock market
crash in the United States. Businesses across the country
were suffering, and many were forced to close their
doors. Unemployment was widespread, especially in the
central prairies, where farmers had also faced two years
of drought and a huge drop in wheat prices, creating
fewer opportunities in the farming industry. Small towns

became smaller, as farmers and their families began to leave for opportunities elsewhere.

Winnipeg, which had been Canada's third largest city in the 1920s, had lost its ranking to Vancouver. This once vibrant city was beginning to tumble down at an accelerated pace as businesses continued to close and labour unrest ensued.

There were some rumblings that the Winnipeg Medical Society was considering strike action. Many doctors were not being paid for their services, and if they were, they were sometimes being paid in kind, with items such as livestock, poultry, or garden vegetables. The depression left many a man with little or no money to buy food, let alone pay doctors. Doctors could no longer tolerate the fact that hospitals were being paid but they were not; the Winnipeg city government and most rural municipalities covered hospital costs for residents who were unemployed, but this did not cover doctor's bills.

For Louis Mahy's family, 1933 did not exactly start well, either. The municipality, realizing that Louis and Lea's house in Grande Clairière was empty more often than not, advised Louis that he could stay there rent-free for the time being, but that if another family needed the home, he would need to vacate the premises. He wondered how he would tell Lea this and what it would do to her spirit.

That said, the free rent certainly helped Louis pay part of the hospital bills, which were mounting, given the fee

was $1.50 per day. As it was, he was already in arrears
by a month. He was working an average of three days
per week. It was certainly not enough to cover expenses,
but it was something. He was aware that the municipality was covering expenses for residents who couldn't pay
their hospital bills. For now, Louis was trying to keep up
with the bills himself, and he appreciated the help the
municipality offered him by not having to pay rent, if
only for a few weeks or months. Eventually, Louis would
also have to pay fees directly to Dr. Fraser, who had held
back on sending him any invoices at this point.

Though he tried to stay positive, Louis was becoming
frustrated. While he could empathize with the pain his
wife had to bear, he sometimes thought that she wasn't
trying hard enough to get her energy level up.

Why was she still lying in bed every time he went to
see her? Why wouldn't she even try to sit up? Or stand?
Or walk?

And he worried that when she did get up, she would
find it difficult to ever get back to the stamina she had
had before her illness.

Louis had spoken to a few friends who had been to
Winnipeg and came back with some interesting findings. A small population from Belgium now lived in
Saint-Boniface, a predominantly French community
across the Red River from Winnipeg. They boasted
about the excellent care patients received at Saint-
Boniface Hospital. This hospital was the largest in the

Winnipeg surrounding area. It was a teaching facility with an impeccable reputation. These same friends had offered Louis free board and room, if he could get Lea to Saint-Boniface. There, perhaps, she would receive better care and have a better chance at survival. Louis had not really kept up with any news of an impending strike by Winnipeg doctors, but had been warned that this could cause issues in transferring Lea to the big city. Still, he hung onto the idea and told Lea all about it on his next Sunday visit.

CHAPTER 6

February 1933

February 12, 1933

Dear Louis,

I received your letter the day before yesterday. You ask me if I will try to get up next week. If my temperature doesn't rise again, I think yes. Eight days ago, I had a terrible setback... my stomach bloated and my fever went way up, and from Saturday to Tuesday, a lot of pus was escaping from this one tiny hole on my abdomen. This has caused some delays with my recovery. My wounds were closing so nicely before this and I thought I would be allowed to get up and move around, but now the abscess is so irritated. There is only a very thin layer of skin left. As for me returning home, there is no use even thinking about it. In the condition I am now, we would need to hire a good nurse and even then, I'm not sure that my mother would be able to handle it. Some days, I'm being cared for night and day. You wouldn't believe what they have to do to me every day... the change of linens and clothing and all. It's bad enough that I'm sick, let alone getting others sick.

As for going to Saint-Boniface Hospital, do as you like, but I am afraid of the drive down there. I would need to have a nurse with me all the way there. If you decide you want to bring me to Saint-Boniface, please bring my rosary.

You asked me if I bought more wine. No, I haven't but the nurses have been giving me another wine that they say is better for me. I've asked them to buy some iron wine for me many times, but they keep forgetting. I've stopped asking. I hope you are doing well. That's all for today. As always, hugs to Jean and Maurice for me... my two poor little ones.

Lea, who loves you always

PS. Dr. Fraser isn't back yet. He is studying in Rochester for two weeks. I am hoping to see your mother this week. Could you have her bring me some little breads from the Michaud's?

Nurse Edna knew that the last three weeks had been excruciating for Lea, even though her patient barely complained. Lea had a bout of high fever and abdomen distension, both caused by the ongoing, severe infection at the surgical incision site. As well, months of bed rest was starting to take its toll on Lea's body. Pressure wounds were evident, the patient was barely able to sit up, and she seemed to be getting weaker daily. Just having visitors exhausted her.

Edna worried about how Lea would ever pull through this latest bout of complications. She was relieved to hear that the x-rays to determine if Lea had lung and intestinal tuberculosis had come back negative, but did worry about the results of the tuberculin test, even though it was inconclusive. She had overheard Dr. Fraser speak to the head nurse about the possibility of Lea going to the sanatorium for tuberculosis patients in Ninette. Edna wondered why she would be sent there if she didn't have the disease, and more importantly, how Lea could possibly survive the long ride to get there, given her weakened condition.

In the meantime, it was Nurse Edna's responsibility to ensure that her patient was as comfortable as she could be. On her last visit to Grant's Pharmacy, she picked up the beef and iron wine Lea had been asking her to purchase. Nurse Edna knew that it would be better if Lea took medicine more specific to her particular case, those prescribed by Dr. Fraser, but she also understood the comfort that Lea had in taking iron wine. If nothing else, the concoction might help Lea sleep better at night.

Over the past few months, Lea and the young nurse had become quite close, even though Edna had been cautioned not to befriend patients in her care. Nevertheless, it happened, and the two were kindred spirits, talking about anything and everything every chance they got. They shared stories about the excitement of falling in love and the joys of motherhood. They spoke of sorrowful times as well, how illness can take away those you love and shatter lives in an instant. Edna thought about how she would miss seeing Lea every day once she left Souris Hospital. She hoped that when Lea did leave, it would be under good circumstances. Edna hoped that eventually Lea would go back to her home Grand Clairière to be with her husband and young boys. One thing Edna knew for sure was that as long as Lea was alive, they would remain friends.

February 18, 1933

Chère Maman,

I received your letter yesterday. You tell me that you don't hear of my news very often, but I have never gone a week without writing you. I am, as always about the same. I feel strong enough, but my wounds continue to leak. The doctor tells me that my fever is causing this. It seems as though the various treatments they

*have given me just make the wounds leak
more, not less. What flows out is sometimes
very disgusting. I don't expect that I will
be able to get out of bed again this week. As
long as the wounds are leaking this much, it
is impossible.*

*You tell me you are sewing an outfit for Jean
and that I would laugh if I saw it. No matter
what it looks like, I so appreciate you doing
this. If it weren't for you caring for my dear
little ones this winter, who knows what would
have happened! I sometimes wonder if I will
really, ever heal from this. It was exactly four
months yesterday since I've been here, on my
back, away from my family. Please give kisses
to my poor little ones for me. I await your visit
next week and will be so happy to see you.*

*Your daughter, who will never forget all that
you have done for me,*

Lea

*PS. Please pass my letter on to Louis. I will try
to write him on Wednesday.*

Before beginning to write her next letter, Lea reread
the last one she had received from her mother. She sensed
that something was amiss. It was not so much what her
mother said, but what she didn't say. As always, Maman
mentioned the boys, how they were growing and all, and
that they both needed new clothes. She talked about only
having the time to sew after the boys were in bed, and

by then, she was tired and made silly mistakes. She then went on to say that the weather was dreadfully cold, but she would still try to get over to visit her next week with Lea's oldest sister, Roseanna.

Though she mentioned nothing in the letters, Lea sensed that everyday life was becoming a struggle for Sylvie. Lea knew her mother. She knew that she was a woman with a lot of energy. But she also knew that everyone had their limitations. Lea realized that spending the last four months caring for two toddlers must most certainly be taking its toll on her mother. And when Maman was tired, which wasn't often, it was obvious. It showed in her eyes and her facial expression.

Lea thought back to when she was a young girl, being raised in a large family, with many of her siblings still living at home. Maman would be up at the crack of dawn, already washed and dressed by the time Joseph or any of the children were out of bed, and she was always eager to tackle the day ahead. In the winter, Lea's father and brothers handled most of the outdoor chores and Maman spent most of her time inside, cleaning, cooking, baking, sewing clothes for all her children, and teaching her young daughters to do the same. When nicer weather arrived, she would plant and take care of a large vegetable garden. When the vegetables were ready for picking, she spent hours doing so with a skip in her step, and later canned many jars of pickled cucumbers, beans and beets.

Lea could remember returning from Maple Hill School, just three miles west of their home, and always seeing both her parents hard at work. This was the reality of life on a farm. There was always something to be done. Once school was out for the summer, Maman would round up the children and assign outside chores. The boys of the family would handle the tasks that required heavy lifting or pulling. The girls did gardening and took care of the animals. Most days, if the weather cooperated, the family would be outdoors from morning until early evening. Then, they would gather around their large kitchen table for a huge meal. Sylvie made her own sausages, often using meat from deer that Joseph and the boys hunted, and she cooked delicious beef and vegetable stews. The stew would sit all day on the woodstove, and the aroma was delectable. Lea sometimes wondered how her mother managed to do it all, all the time.

When Lea's parents separated, her mother was determined to thrive on her own and took on most household chores inside and out. By then, many of the children were gone, but there was still much to be done. In the spring, as soon as the snow started to melt, Maman spent a good portion of her days working on her land. There were animal shelters to clean from the long, rugged winter, a large yard to maintain, and a garden to till.

Lea was so grateful to her mother for taking care of Jean and Maurice. Without her help, the boys would not have been able to stay together. Her sisters had all offered to care for the children, but many of them had young children of their own, or were expecting. There was also the financial burden of having an extra mouth to feed. Maman opened her home and her heart to the young boys and to Louis as well at times, and seemed to be glad to do so. Still, Lea worried about her. She seemed to be losing some of her steam, and her temperament was beginning to change. She seemed flustered at times, and impatient. Lea also noticed on Maman's last visit that she walked slowly, with a bit of a limp, and her face seemed flushed. Lea vowed to be more attentive to Maman's demeanour on her next visit.

Lea wrote the date to start her next letter and realized that Louis' birthday was but two days away. She suddenly felt terrible that this hadn't occurred to her sooner. Was she so wrapped up in her own self-pity that she put aside anything else that may have been significant in her life? Under normal circumstances, Lea would have fussed incessantly in preparation for her husband's birthday. She would have baked a cake, perhaps put up a decoration or two, and likely planned a small supper with family members. But this was not to be this year.

Lea knew that Louis would likely be visiting her the next day, and she thought of what she could do to celebrate her husband's thirty-seventh birthday at the hospital. She would need to get the nurses to help her. She would have loved to have the ability to step outside for just one day! Then, they could have walked just a few steps over from the hospital to the swinging bridge. Of course, Lea would not have been able to walk across the over six hundred feet of cable, but the view would have been wonderful just the same. It would have been romantic, something Lea hadn't felt in a very long time. Unfortunately, after four months in hospital, she was still confined to a bed.

Just as Lea thought about what she could do to surprise her husband, one of the nurses walked in with some fresh, homemade bread from Mme. Michaud in Grande Clairière. What a pleasant surprise! M. Pallard had driven to Souris on other matters earlier in the day, and stopped in to drop this treat off especially for Lea, care of Louis' mother. She also sent a small envelope containing pink glass rosary beads. Lea had thought about asking for these months ago. She was glad that she finally mentioned it to Louis in her last letter, and was sure that he likely passed the message on to his mother. Ill health prevented her mother-in-law from visiting in person, but the kind woman jumped at the chance of sending this with M. Pallard, when she knew he was heading to Souris.

How sweet of her, thought Lea. And how fortuitous. The bread was the closest she would be able to get to a birthday cake for Louis. She could cover a thick piece of bread with one of his favourite jams, either strawberry-rhubarb or saskatoon berry, from one of the many jars she had received from well-meaning visitors. All she needed was a candle. She'd seen the hospital staff walk around with white enamel candlestick holders at night to check on the patients. She was sure that the nurses would let her borrow a candle for this special occasion.

Luckily, Lea had done some planning well ahead of time. After not having been able to buy her husband a Christmas present, she made sure to order something for his birthday from the Army & Navy mail order store in Regina. She had found an advertisement while reading a copy of the Souris Plaindealer. She knew Louis would appreciate a warm pair of horsehide pullover mitts. They were on sale for forty-four cents. She also purchased two ear-band wool hats for her sons. At forty-eight cents apiece, they were a little expensive, but Lea thought this was well worth it with the cold prairie winters Manitobans had to endure. She was able to pay for these items with the money her mother had sent her just before Christmas. She arranged for her order to be sent to her at Souris Hospital. She knew the boys often travelled by horse and sleigh, and these hats would provide the warmth they needed. After buying the iron wine, this only left Lea with ten cents, but she was pleased with her purchases and thought Maman would completely understand why she spent her money so frivolously.

Worry turned to excitement, as Lea thought less about her mother's health and more about the birthday plans for Louis. She hoped that Louis would come alone by sleigh. If he skipped going to church, which he often did anyway, he could leave early in the morning, as soon as the sun came up. If he hopped a ride with the parish priest, they would not arrive before one o'clock, and only then if they left right after Sunday mass.

By sleigh, he could get there much earlier, and they would be alone for the entire afternoon. It's not that she wasn't grateful for Father Bertrand's visits; she just wanted more time alone with her husband on his birthday. In any case, Lea could not wait for Louis to arrive. She had one of the evening nurses help her wrap Louis' gift in newspaper wrapping and tied a yellow ribbon she had saved from a box of chocolates Louis had given her. She fell asleep that night with a smile, looking forward to seeing the love of her life the next day.

That night, Lea dreamt of better times. At one point during the night, she woke up and found herself reminiscing about a family gathering last summer at Maman's house. Maurice was just a tiny baby, no more than two months old, and her sisters and nieces were passing him back and forth, taking their turns to coddle the young infant. Jean was playing with other young cousins and completely enjoying the attention from his extended family. Louis and Lea took advantage of being able to spend time together, while others looked after their children. As the gramophone played Lucienne Boyer, Louis led Lea to the middle of the living room floor and they danced torso to torso, cheek to cheek.

Parlez moi d'amour
Redites-moi des choses tendres
Votre beau discours
Mon coeur n'est pas las de l'entendre
... Je vous aime

Louis wasn't particularly fond of dancing, but he knew that Lea loved it, so he obliged her often. Though they had already been married over three years, Louis and Lea still felt like newlyweds. They were still smitten, always enjoyed each other's company, and still revelled in finding out new things about each other.

After their dance, they snuck outside and walked around the fields and enjoyed a bit of time by themselves. Drought and grasshoppers aside, this was still a part of the world that held a lot of hope. They imagined possibly buying Sylvie's land from her one day. Being the last one to leave home, Lea had at one time talked about that option with her mother. Sylvie knew very well that a time would come when the farm would become too much for her. Of course, Maman would still live with them, but Louis and Lea could take over the farm business. Then perhaps, eventually, Louis could stop working for the railway and work closer to home. And until he did, Sylvie would be great help with the boys. Yes, their future had indeed seemed bright.

When Lea woke up, she did not open her eyes for a moment, trying to stay in her wonderful dreams of better times. But then reality struck. She felt feverish again, and her incision was throbbing. For the last few days, she'd felt as though she was developing a cold, and now, her chest felt congested. All she could hope for to make her day go well was to have Louis arrive, as he usually did every Sunday.

February, 1933 had been horrendously cold—minus twenties and thirties most days—but this particular Sunday had warmed up somewhat. Though still below freezing, it was warm enough for Louis to take a ride to Souris by horse and sleigh. The skies were cloudy, however, and a dusting of snow hampered the ride a bit on the way down, delaying him a bit. He arrived at the hospital around one o'clock, only to find his wife sleeping.

Louis gently nudged Lea and kissed her forehead. Slowly, she opened her eyes.

"You made it!"

"Yes, I did. I try not to miss a Sunday, if I can. How are you?"

"Uncomfortable. I have a bit of a chest cold today. But never mind that. I have something for you!"

Lea proceeded to have Louis open the door to her side table. There, he found a piece of bread on a small plate, covered in jam, with a huge candle smack dab in the middle of it. The white candle was about an inch in diameter, taking a good chunk out of the middle of the four-inch-square piece of bread.

It was the ugliest thing he had ever seen.

He loved it!

Beside the make-shift birthday cake was a half-bottle of leftover dandelion wine and two clean glasses from the hospital kitchen.

"It's your birthday tomorrow. We need to celebrate."

Louis simply smiled and gazed at his beautiful wife. Even after all this time in the hospital where this illness had ravaged her, she still looked stunning in his eyes. How caring, he thought, that she had done this. He had no words.

"I dreamt of you yesterday. I was recalling the party at Maman's house last July. Remember? When we danced and took a walk through the fields? I miss dancing with you, Louis. And taking walks with you. And spending time with you and the boys."

They talked nostalgically about that day. A day that now seemed so long ago. They laughed at the fact that, at the end of the evening, having both imbibed a few too many, they left for home and realized a mile out that they had left the children behind. They ran back to find both Jean and Maurice were sound asleep and nestled comfortably on their grandmother's bed, where they had been most of the evening. Sylvie told the young lovers to go on without the boys and come back to get them in the morning. They reminisced about the good times of that particular evening, but both Louis and Lea chose not to mention what they spoke of that evening in the field. The dream to purchase Maman's land now seemed so unattainable.

Lea then had Louis reach under the hospital bed for the gifts for him and the boys. Louis opened the package with the yellow ribbon. In it, he found the grey mitts and immediately tried them on. Then, with the mitts still on his hands, he held his wife's face, pulled her closer to his and told her how much he loved her.

They talked more that Sunday than they had in a long time, reminiscing about their early days together and how they could be happy again, if only she could recover. Soon, Louis realized that the afternoon was nearly over and he would need to head back to Grande Clairière. As it was, he would likely be driving the last leg of the trip in darkness.

As Louis prepared to leave, he turned to Lea and said, "I don't think I could go on living if you don't make it through this, Lea."

"No. Don't say that, Louis. You can't think that way." She grabbed his arm, pulled him toward her and wrapped her other arm around him as best she could, feeling the pull on her wounds. How frustrated she felt at that particular moment that she was unable to get out of bed to embrace her husband. They held onto each other and said nothing more. They both sobbed. The pain Lea now felt was mostly in her heart.

They vowed they would write each other at least once the following week, and Louis promised he would be back next Sunday.

Regrettably, Lea's cold really weakened her, and she was barely able to sit up for an entire week, let alone write. As for Louis, he too caught a cold and was unable to write or visit her the following week.

February 27, 1933

Chère Maman,

I am doing fairly well, as always, just as you saw last week. The wounds are still leaking a lot and this is beginning to bother me. I fear it will never stop. It seems to be warming up outside. Perhaps we will have an early spring. I would love to return home when the weather improves. Maybe the hospital will discharge me if they know Mrs. Hardy will take care of me. Just in case, I am starting to get rid of items in my room. I finished the pie you brought me last week and have one little bread left, which I will finish today. Was Maurice happy to see you and Roseanna when you returned home? I'm sure he was. Please give Jean and Maurice big hugs and kisses from me.

Your daughter who thinks of you often,
Lea

A week before penning this letter, Lea received a lovely visit from her mother and her oldest sister, Roseanna. Maman brought a delicious apple pie and a few more little breads from Mme. Michaud. Lea was glad to hear that Roseanna, whose children were all grown up now, had been spending many days with Maman, to help care for the boys. Roseanna told Lea she was developing a close connection with baby Maurice, and he was attached to her as well. Lea felt quite relieved that the burden was no longer strictly on her mother to care for the boys. She could see that Maman had perked up a bit since the last time she saw her. Her sisters and their families had been so generous, each of them taking their turns to help out. Once again, Lea was so thankful.

Lea talked to her mother and sister about Louis' last visit. She told them about the fun they had celebrating his birthday, but also expressed how worried she was about her husband.

"He is starting to lose faith, Maman. He seemed so fragile."

She asked that they both look out for him and encourage him when possible. They promised they would. They had both heard that he was spending more time at the pool hall, where he sat alone in a corner and drank. Neither chose to tell Lea that.

Her sister had a bit of good news, though. She told Lea that Anna Hardy had offered to take care of Lea at home if the hospital thought to discharge her. This news left Lea thinking more and more about going home. Her next door neighbour had offered to care for her, how opportune! Would her doctor discharge her if he knew this? Could this be possible? All she could do was hope. She was anxious to speak to Louis about it and see what his thoughts were. Surely, going back home to Grande Clairière would be better than going all the way to Saint-Boniface for care. For the first time in a very long time, Lea was truly hopeful.

February 27, 1933

Cher Louis,

A few words to tell you that everything is about the same... always leaking... always the same news. I would love to go home, but other times I think to myself that I might be better here. Perhaps when the weather improves, if Mrs. Hardy is still offering to take care of me, I could go home and I'd be in good hands. Only she would offer something as generous as this! It's funny, for nearly five months now I've been telling you the same thing and nothing seems to ever change. I have nothing new to tell you. I am on my back most of the time, with nothing to see or do. I only sit up to eat.

As always, give kisses to Jean and Maurice for me.

Lea, who thinks of you often

PS. The doctor just came to see me and he has told me something that will cause you much sorrow, as it has me. Louis, he says there is no cure for what I have. He told me that they found tuberculosis in my wounds. He would like to bring me to Ninette Sanatorium when spring arrives. I asked if I could go right away, if I could get better care there, but he doesn't think I am strong enough to make the trip.

Louis, you must find a way to get through this. You have two little boys that belong to you. My poor Louis. My poor dear little ones. After all these months of hoping and praying, it looks as though I will be leaving you after all. I must stop writing now. I can no longer see the lines on the paper.

Sitting in a black leather chair at the Rural Municipality of Cameron office in Hartney, Louis was visibly uncomfortable. He stared across a large oak desk to where the reeve of the municipality was seated. Neither of them seemed to want to be the first to speak.

"We know of a local family who is in need of the house, Louis. You must vacate by April first."

After a long pause, Louis muttered "That's actually quite fine. We've just been given some news that my wife may need to be transferred to the sanatorium in Ninette when the weather warms up."

The reeve cleared his throat, not really knowing what to say.

"I'm sorry to hear that," was all that came out.

"I will be living at my mother-in-law's place for now. That's where my children are. For the time being, that is the best scenario. And if Lea... um... *once* Lea returns home, we will need to get back on our feet before we think about getting a place of our own again."

The two men shook hands, and Louis shuffled out of the office.

Well, that's done, thought Louis. Now, how was he going to tell Lea?

By the time Louis made it back to Grande Clairière from Hartney, reality was setting in. He would need to move out of the place that had held so much hope for him and Lea, a place that Lea had lovingly converted to a beautiful and comfortable home for the two of them and their little boys. It broke his heart.

Refusing to feel sorry for himself, he turned his thoughts to some more practical issues. He walked around in each of the rooms and realized that he would need to pack a lot of things. Though some of the furniture belonged with the house, there were a number of items that would need to be moved—two dressers, a desk, a few chairs, wall hangings, books, oil lamps and candleholders, and many kitchen items. Suddenly, he became overwhelmed at the thought of it.

Luckily, he had brought little Jean's bed and baby Maurice's crib to Sylvie's before Christmas. When Lea'd had a bad spell in December, it seemed the wise thing to do. Most of the children's clothes were also at Sylvie's, as well as their box of toys. And then there was the food stored in the outdoor shed. There was just too much to think about, and, as anxiety mounted, he shifted his thoughts to something else.

Instead, he tried to figure out when he would next be able to make it to Souris to let Lea know. For the first time in months, he had work lined up every day of the week. He decided to take a train out to Souris on Saturday morning. That way, he could spend the day with Lea and they could talk about the move.

The more he thought of it, the more he struggled with how he would tell Lea. Of course, she knew the inevitability that it would happen one day, but now they had an actual date, April first. Louis felt an actual physical pain in the pit of his stomach.

Later in the evening, after calming himself with a few shots of home brew, Louis thought back to his previous visit, the day before his birthday. They had had such a good visit, and even though he was struck with sadness that he may lose her one day, he came home feeling optimistic, and thinking much of his life would improve if Lea's health would return. And after the beautiful day they had spent together, he'd felt this was a real possibility. He was enthused at the prospect that his wife could come back home and convalesce near her family, with the help of Mrs. Hardy and Lea's mother and siblings. His young sons would be happier, back in the arms of their mother. They could all resume the good life they once had and get back on their feet again.

And then, just a week later, he received this woeful letter and its postscript. And all he could do was repeat the words to that familiar song.

Life is sometimes too bitter,
if we don't believe in the figments of our imagination.
Sadness can be quickly soothed and taken away by a kiss.
From the heart, wounds can be mended,
by a discourse of reassuring words

CHAPTER 7

March 1933

March 4, 1933

Cher Louis,

I thought I would have received a letter from you yesterday, but I didn't. What do you think of me going to Ninette? I really believe that even if there is only a slim chance for me to recover by going there, I should still take that chance. I spoke to the doctor again today and he told me he would want to drive me there with his car in early April. He thinks it will be impossible for me to make the trip by train all the way to Ninette. I am now wondering if Maman will be able to continue to look after the dear little ones. Poor Jean, who keeps asking to come and see me so I could spoil him. (Now, I will be so much further away.) And my little Maurice, will he ever have the opportunity to be spoiled by his mother? My two darling children... I cry for them every day, even though it doesn't help the situation.

That is all for today. Hugs and kisses, as always, to Jean and Maurice.

Thinking of you,
Lea

Lea was bothered that she hadn't seen or heard from Louis in almost two weeks. She had been told by visiting family members that he'd been scheduled on a huge maintenance job in eastern Saskatchewan, and though he came home every night, his days were long and arduous. Lea knew it was impossible for him to visit her, but he could at least have written a letter or two.

By the time she finished writing her letter and set the pencil down, Louis walked into the room. He held a small bouquet of pink carnations. Any thoughts of anger dissipated as he handed her the flowers and kissed her on her forehead. What point would there be in showing disappointment?

"Where were you ever able to find fresh flowers at this time of year?" questioned Lea.

"The ladies auxiliary received a small shipment from Winnipeg yesterday and were selling them downstairs just as I arrived," replied Louis. "Did you know that pink carnations are thought to have first appeared on earth in the time of Jesus?" he asked. "The belief is that they were made from the virgin mother's tears. As such, to this day, carnations are a symbol of a mother's undying love for her children. My mother told me this."

Lea smiled and thanked him for being so thoughtful. She wondered if Louis himself really believed what he had just told her. She wasn't sure if she should believe it herself, but she liked the symbolism. She would look at the carnations each and every day and think of her young sons, and Louis.

They spent the entire day talking. Louis wasted no time in telling her that the municipality knew of a family who needed their house. Lea was a little surprised, but after the confirmation that she was going to be admitted to Ninette, she knew that keeping the house would have been impossible. She worried about the burden of additional work that the move would put on Louis. He assured her that many family members had already offered to help, and he would be fine.

They talked about when she might actually be going to Ninette. Lea told Louis that Dr. Fraser had thought she might be able to go sooner if the weather forecast proved to be correct. She also told him that the doctor had explained to her that, while the x-rays did not reveal any signs of tuberculosis on either her lungs or her intestines, the tuberculin test, where liquid was injected into her forearm, did. It caused her skin to turn red and rise slightly. That, combined with the delayed wound healing, was enough for Dr. Fraser to contact his colleagues at Ninette and make arrangements to have her transferred. "As soon as there is a day above freezing, Dr. Fraser will take me there. It could be as soon as next week."

They talked about what items would need to be moved from the hospital. Louis checked out the drawers on the side table to see its contents and assess what should be kept, sent to Ninette, brought home, or discarded.

"My new watch… back home. It doesn't work."

"Nightgowns from home… to Ninette. I might finally get to wear them over there," hoped Lea.

"Matches… to Ninette. You never know when we might need to light a candle for another birthday cake," she said, and they giggled quietly. They made decisions on the spot and laughed at their efficiency.

"I want to keep all the letters you and the family have sent me," Lea said sternly as she held the large pile. She told him that she read them over and over again to make the time pass by. Louis understood.

Lastly, they talked about whether Lea's mother would still be able to look after Jean and Maurice. As soon as the boys' names were mentioned, Lea's eyes filled with tears.

And then, the words stopped. They both sat quietly, staring at the walls, at the ground, or sometimes in each other's eyes. After what seemed like an extremely long time, Louis finally said that he had already discussed this with her mother, and Sylvie felt strong enough to continue to look after the boys. Lea's sisters were helping more lately, each taking turns spending some time at Maman's house. He reassured Lea that she needn't worry about the boys. They were fine.

Still, Lea stayed quiet. Thoughts of her sons rolled through her head and she continued to weep ever so faintly. Finally, she gathered up the strength to say the last thing she would say for the rest of their visit.

"I will be so much further now; I may never see them again."

As Louis sat on the train back to Grande Clairière, those words played in his mind over and over and over again.

"So, did Dr. Fraser tell you that he wants to take me to the sanatorium in Ninette? What do you think about it?" Lea stared intently at Nurse Edna.

Nurse Edna had a dejected look on her face. "Oh, Lea, I trust wholeheartedly that Dr. Fraser is recommending what is best for you. Ninette is a fine facility and is the perfect place for you. It has everything you need to give you any chance at a complete recovery."

Lea knew that the divide between Edna's words and sad facial expression had to do with the fact that they would miss each other's company. In the last four months, Lea and Edna had become friends, and Lea worried about how she would do without one of the positive influences in her life at Souris Hospital. But she also knew that it was best if she followed her doctor's advice.

Though Edna didn't let on, she did have some concerns about Lea going to Ninette, but the nurse's apprehension had nothing to do with the excellence of the facility. The sanatorium was built at the start of the century to tackle the tuberculosis epidemic in Manitoba. It was the first of its kind in the Prairie provinces and it had a great reputation. Her concern had more to do with the diagnosis of her patient, her friend.

Dr. Fraser had been conferring on a regular basis with both the Medical Superintendent and his assistant at Ninette. He had also been hell bent on the idea of sending her there, especially since he had returned from Rochester. Based on the results of a second tuberculin test, it was agreed that there was a possibility that the patient had intestinal tuberculosis. Though this was a rare form of the disease, it was not unheard of in these parts, and if it was indeed the correct diagnosis, then Ninette Sanatorium would be the best place for her.

"I've heard many good things about Ninette," Edna reassured her. "You will be in good hands there. A nurse from my graduating class is working there now. With any luck, you may get to know her."

"It just won't be the same without you at my side, Edna."

"Don't worry. I will do my best to visit you."

"I will be so much further away now from the boys. I don't even know if Louis will be able to visit as often. It's such a long way from Grande Clairière."

"Your boys are in good hands, Lea. And you can rest assured that Louis will make every effort to visit you just as often in Ninette."

"I hope so. I just hope this is the right decision for me and my family," Lea said as tears streamed down her face.

Edna stepped out of the room and let out a sigh. If there is a God, thought Edna, now would be a time to call upon him for compassion and fortitude.

March 11, 1933

Cher Louis,

A few lines to let you know that I am doing well enough but my strength does not seem to be coming back quickly. I am eating well enough. I hope this nice weather continues for the next week. (Maybe the doctor will then consider driving me to Ninette.) I think it is still snowing at night though. I don't have much to say because it seems to be the same thing every day. I hope that the two little ones and the rest of the family are in good health.

Please give hugs to the dear little ones for me and kisses to you as well.

Lea, who thinks of you all so often

Just as Lea was placing her letter to Louis in an envelope, Dr. Fraser walked in her room.

"Well, today is the day!" he exclaimed. "Today, I will take you to Ninette."

Though the temperature was still below freezing, Dr. Fraser was confident that his patient would be kept warm enough in his fairly new automobile, a 1929 Hudson four-door sedan. He had purchased it a few years back from Andy Murray in Souris and was one of the first in town to have a winter-proofed vehicle. It was completely enclosed, with a glass windshield. It also had wide, comfortable seats. He was sure that if Lea was wrapped in blankets and kept warm, she would make the one and a half hour drive to Ninette without any complications. He was a bit concerned about her worsening cold symptoms, but he would have hospital staff apply a good amount of poultice to cover the patient's chest and keep her comfortable.

Dr. Fraser was absolutely certain that admitting Lea Mahy to Ninette Sanatorium was the best possible option, given the circumstances. On his recent trip to the Mayo Clinic, he conferred with other doctors about this case, and then came to the conclusion that the transfer was the best thing for his patient. Souris Hospital had done all it could to help her. There was nothing more she needed in terms of care but rest and time to heal. Ninette could offer her that. Souris could not. Souris could no longer afford to look after her.

Lea wasn't sure if she should put on a smile or break into tears. Physically, she didn't feel up to the challenge

of getting into a vehicle and taking a fifty mile drive in
what was essentially still a chilly winter day. Her chest
was congested and she had a dry cough and a low fever.
But she decided she had no choice but to go along with
what her doctor wanted her to do. She made arrangements to call Pallard's store in Grande Clairière. They
could get a message over to her mother and Louis.

Luckily, Louis had taken most of Lea's belongings
with him back to Grande Clairière on his last visit. The
nursing staff packed what remained in her small leather
suitcase. One by one, personnel at Souris Hospital who
had come to know Lea over the last five months came
to bid her farewell. Edna was not there that day. Lea
thought that might have been a blessing from above. She
knew that their goodbye would have been an emotional
one. It was just as well that they didn't see each other.

After lunch, an orderly was called upon to carry Lea
down the stairs to the first floor of the hospital, place her
in a wheelchair and take her to the verandah. The second
Lea was brought outside, the sun saturated her eyes,
causing her to lose her sight for a moment. Having spent
such a long time in a room with only a small window,
she was no longer used to the vivid intensity of the sun
shining directly down on her. Next, her lungs filled with
crisp, cold air. It was frightening and invigorating all at
the same time.

Dr. Fraser stood by his car near the front of the hospital. He looked much more casual than Lea had ever

seen before. He wore a beige wool cap, a brown tweed coat and his round, silver eyeglasses were replaced with a pair of black aviator sunglasses. When he saw Lea, he hopped up the steps, and between he and the orderly, they brought her to the vehicle and placed Lea in the back seat, trying to make her as comfortable as possible. They propped her up with a few feather pillows and wrapped her in blankets. The orderly placed her suitcase beside her and handed her the March issue of the Ladies' Home Journal to read on the ride down. She smiled and thanked him. Looking down at the magazine, with the front cover depicting a well-to-do couple dressed to the nines, Lea thought it highly improbable that anything in this magazine would really interest her. Still, she thought it was so very kind of the orderly to do that for her.

Dr. Fraser hopped in the driver's seat and off they went. A few staff members stood at the hospital doorway, waving as Dr. Fraser began to drive away. Lea wiped a few tears as they drove by the swinging bridge. Soon, they were driving over the Souris River and headed down to the newly built provincial Highway 2 to Ninette. The gravel road still had a bit of snow on it, but travelling was less bumpy than Dr. Fraser had anticipated.

Unexpectedly, Lea rather enjoyed her voyage down to the sanatorium. She hadn't seen the outdoors in such a long time. She marvelled at the miles and miles of flat land set against the light blue sky, a view only possible on the prairies. She gazed across snow-covered fields where she could see the horizon clear across the land-scape. She couldn't help but think that the view looked like a masterful painting. The odd time, hills sprung up, as did scatterings of aspen and oak, stripped of their leaves. A few times over the course of the trip, they saw herds of cattle, but most of the time, only the vast fields of Manitoba could be seen every direction. The farther east they drove, the more the sky accumulated loads of billowy clouds, which added to the spectacular view.

Dr. Fraser could see in his rear-view mirror that Lea was enjoying the ride immensely, so he kept conversation to a minimum. He saw her demeanor change from downhearted to quietly optimistic as the winter roads led them closer to Ninette.

As they turned onto Highway 18, they began to see evergreens now and again, full of bristled pines and cones. Their deep green colour was a great contrast against the deep blue sky. Lea smiled at the visions passing by her, outdoor scenery that she had not seen in a very long time.

Before they knew it, they were driving edging up to the small town of Ninette and found their way to a winding road which led them to their final destination.

The Ninette Sanatorium was a series of buildings built in a rural setting in southwestern Manitoba, on the banks of Pelican Lake. Each of the buildings had its own purpose. The first building to the left upon arrival was the administration building. Dr. Fraser pulled his car just alongside the building and told Lea to wait in the car while he ran in to let the staff know they had arrived. While waiting, Lea surveyed the premises. She marvelled at the sheer number of buildings on the site. Most were situated on hilltops. All were nestled among trees, shrubs, and other foliage, and they looked… charming. Modern, red-roofed buildings in a cottage-like setting. It was all quite soothing.

Lea wondered if either of the two larger hospices up the hill behind the main building was the women's infirmary. She could see that there were people sitting in screened-in porches on the second floor of both buildings, but couldn't make out if they were men or women. Those balconies, which were on most buildings, were *enormous*. She wondered if she would ever get the opportunity to spend any time on them.

And she wondered if she would know anybody. She wondered what the staff would be like. She wondered if her nurses would be as comforting to her as Edna had been.

She hoped for it.

Dr. Fraser leaped back in the vehicle and said, "We are heading over to the West Infirmary. You will have a beautiful view from there, Lea. I guarantee it."

As they drove up, Lea caught a glimpse of the lake. Much of it was still frozen, but she was able to see small scattered patches of water and marshland. When they reached the front doors of the infirmary, they were greeted by an older man who helped Dr. Fraser place Lea into a wheelchair. Before bringing Lea inside, the friendly looking man turned the chair away from the building, looked at Lea and pointed ahead. It was high noon, and the sun was beating directly down onto her face. Even though it was still cold out, she could feel the warmth of the sun touch down upon her cheeks. She immediately saw the magnificence of the lake, even though it was mostly still frozen. She had not anticipated it to be so widespread, and after being cooped up in a small hospital room for almost five months, it was a sight to behold. The waters curved towards a bank filled with tall oak and birch trees, creating a picturesque landscape. Lea took a deep breath and simply enjoyed the view. And then what amazed her was that the air that filled her lungs felt so incredibly fresh… cold, but fresh. She hadn't had the opportunity to breath outside air in a very long time. She basked in the glory of being outside in this secluded corner of the world. For a good minute, Lea closed her eyes and tilted her head toward the sky, soaking in the purity of the outdoors. She wished she could be left there at that very spot for the rest of the day.

Instead, the older man turned Lea towards the huge wooden door and wheeled her inside the West Infirmary. There, they were greeted by Harriet, who Lea would soon find out was her new matter-of-fact nurse with a heart of gold. Harriet told Dr. Fraser she could take over from here. Dr. Fraser insisted on going up to Lea's room, saying he would like to carry her belongings up and see to it that she was left there in good condition. He also planned to meet with Dr. Ross, who would be Lea's new doctor. Lea smiled at the undivided attention she was getting from her doctor and her new nurse.

They went over to the back of the building where a lift elevator brought them to the third floor. Lea had only ever been in an elevator at Eaton's in Winnipeg. This one was less glamorous—in fact, it was a bit rickety—but it did its job and slowly lifted them to the third level. Once off the elevator, they headed down a long well-lit hallway with shiny white, orange, and turquoise floor tiles. They turned right into the second-last room on the floor. There were two beds. A small stuffed bear with a big red bow and a few pieces of mail sat on the one nearest to the door. Lea wished this was her bed; the next best thing to writing letters was receiving them.

"*That* is your bed." said Nurse Harriet, pointing to the bed next to the window. "You are lucky to get such a view! You have a roommate who prefers to be closer to the doorway. She is mobile, so she can go to the bathing and bathroom facilities on her own. That won't be the case for you, my dear. At least not for now."

Lea was amazed at the sheer size of the window, so much larger than the one she had in her room at Souris Hospital. This one was a little wider and much longer, and she would likely be able to see outside, even when lying down!

When Dr. Fraser and Nurse Harriet helped Lea into her bed, they could see how exhausted she was from the drive down. She barely had the force to move her arms and legs, let alone pull herself up.

"I think we should just let you lay here and relax a tad before we put you in bedclothes." said the nurse. "I will take Dr. Fraser over to see Dr. Ross and will be back to help you in about ten minutes. So for now, just rest."

Dr. Fraser turned to Lea, held her shoulders and looked straight into her big blue eyes.

"You are in good hands here, Lea. You will have a new level of care here. This is a mighty fine facility. Here, there is a good chance you can recover." And with that, he left.

Lea observed the room, immediately taking a liking to the mint green walls. Two framed still-life prints adorned the walls above the beds and a small crucifix hung above the door. The more she looked around, the more she noticed some of the niceties now provided to her, most notably, a small clock on the north wall. Lea smiled when she saw it, thinking she would no longer have to rely on watches that don't work half the time. She also soon realized that a modern electrical fixture hung from the ceiling and a receptacle to open and shut the light was installed just beside the door. This was a far cry from the coal-lit lamps used in Souris. Lea marvelled at the fact that this hospital had electric lights throughout. She also noticed a large, rose-coloured velvet chair, and pictured herself sitting comfortably in it once she was able to get up on her own. She soaked in the ambiance of her new *temporary* home and smiled. And yet, something didn't feel quite right. For all its beauty and serenity, the Ninette Sanatorium was miles and miles from Grande Clairière.

The waves washed gently along the shoreline, where two young children sat in the golden sand and played with tin pails and small wooden spoons. The sun was bright as bright could be, and the sky was sapphire blue. Not a cloud in sight. A few steps back, a young couple lay on a quilted blanket, soaking in the rays of the bright warm sun, but always with an eye to the children near them.

Sunshine... outdoors... warmth... family... She wanted this moment to last forever. She relished every second of this glorious day.

"I must go," the man said suddenly. He had a sombre look on his face. "I have to go to work now. I can't visit as often now that you are here. It is too far away."

"But the boys... who will watch over the boys? I cannot get up from this blanket. The doctor told me not to."

"Don't worry. They will be taken care of."

The young woman looked towards the water. The boys were no longer there. All that was left was a rusted tin pail

and an old wooden spoon. "No," she screamed. "Where are
my babies?"

And with that, Lea woke up and realized that
this was the morning of her first night spent at the
Ninette Sanatorium.

On the day Lea had arrived in Ninette, she fell asleep in
the early hours of the evening, without ever even having
met her roommate. The bed next to her stayed empty
most of the next day. Exhausted from the long ride down,
Lea had a late-afternoon nap, waking up only to find out
supper time had passed. By then, a privacy curtain had
been pulled between her and the other bed, and Lea was
just too tired to reach out to her. She had only a bowl of
clear soup, and then went right back to sleep. She slept
well, though she did have a disturbing dream. Lea was
getting used to the fact that nightmares were part of her
life now, especially when she was feverish.

Early the next day, Lea was poked with needles and
given a multitude of tests. The nurses took her temperature and samples of her sputum and urine. Even though
it was a Sunday, a sacred day for Catholics, it was business as usual at the infirmary. No day of rest here. Even
though they had received the x-ray results from Souris
Hospital, they would be taking additional ones of both
her lungs and her intestines. She was scheduled for
x-rays the following day.

The daytime temperature was slightly above freezing. This gave Lea the opportunity to see the outside resting areas for the first time. The balconies were part of every pavilion and cottage on the premises designed for patients. This was so that tuberculosis patients could take advantage of the clean, fresh air of the secluded area, and benefit from the healing powers of nature. Rest was said to be the most important treatment for tuberculosis. It was also believed that six hours of sunshine a day could help in curing this dreaded disease.

Most balconies had three walls made up mostly of large, screened-in, multi-framed windows that let in heat or cold, depending on the time of year, and each spring and summer, patients were treated to lovely breezes from the nearby lake. These sunrooms had a scenic view and each building was unique in its own right, most facing the water, but some with a splendid look at the enchanting grounds. The ceilings were covered in slats of cedar, giving each room a distinct odor of natural wood. The back wall was covered in dull grey panelling and one large wall hanging adorned the centre—a wood frame with nine compartments of glass with fall leaves placed behind five of the panes. Beds filled each balcony, and most patients also had access to a cot. Unfortunately, Lea was not able to lie in a cot, as moving her from her bed could irritate her wounds. After breakfast, Lea was brought down to the second floor in her latch bed, and she was allowed to stay on the outside balcony for about an hour.

Lea was so thankful that she was able to breathe in fresh outside air once again. It was quite cold, however, and she thought how much more comfortable this would become late spring and summer.

Nurses told Lea that she could start to wear her own clothes once she was allowed to go on the balcony on a regular basis. She wasn't sure this would be possible with the wounds on her abdomen still so visibly infected, but wearing one of her own sweaters would be nice after all these months of wearing hospital attire. She jotted down a reminder to ask her mother to clean and send her navy cardigan with Louis on his next visit.

It was late afternoon, two full days after she arrived, before Lea finally met her roommate. Eva was a seventeen year old girl with lung tuberculosis, but after being in the sanatorium for well over two years, she seemed to be on the road to recovery. She spent most of her time on the balcony and was allowed to come and go as she wished. The girl was extremely thin, and had a visible bend in her back. In fact, she walked with a cane. Later, Lea found out that this was because she'd had thoraco-plastic surgery and several of her ribs on her left side were removed. Regardless, she was an extremely pretty girl with hazel eyes, a fair complexion, and wavy red hair. The new roommates barely had a chance to say hello by the time their supper meals arrived.

Lea's first full supper at Ninette was quite the treat. It consisted of a bowl full of chicken soup, veal and ham pie, potatoes and gravy, and a heaping portion of green beans. On a smaller plate, there was a piece of fresh bread and a teaspoon of butter. As well, the tray held a cup of fresh milk and a small piece of matrimonial cake for dessert. Lea was delighted at the variety and the size of the portions. Her eyes were bigger than her stomach however, as she barely ate half of what was given to her.

"Do they always give us great meals like this?" Lea asked her roommate. "This is a lot of food!"

"Yes. Most of the time the food is very good here," Eva replied. "Sometimes, there is too much for me to finish too."

She wondered how often she would have the luxury of eating meat here. What a contrast from Souris, thought Lea. There, she sometimes felt pangs of hunger after eating her lunch or supper. There, she rarely ate meat. Once or twice a week, on average. Lea thought it was best not to relay this information to her new roommate. Certainly, it was the intention of the hospital in Souris to provide good food for their patients, but times were tough and they could only provide what they could afford.

Lea and Eva got acquainted that first evening, but kept the conversations short. Lea still felt quite exhausted—a combination of the travel and a full day of prodding and tests, not to mention the excitement of being in a new place. As much as she felt the urge to write to Louis and tell him about her first two full days at Ninette, she did not have the power to do so.

As she lay in bed, staring at the evening horizon for the first time in a very long time, she wondered if Louis had gotten the message that she had now been transferred. Certainly, he would know by now, she thought. She knew he wouldn't have been able to catch a train on a Sunday, but she had hoped that he could maybe find a ride with someone who owned a vehicle. Regrettably, Sunday came and went without one visitor.

Once again, Lea slept soundly, though she did have a hard time getting to sleep. Thoughts of how far away she was from home and how much she missed her boys occupied her mind.

The next morning, as soon as Lea saw the morning nurse, she received a message that Louis had called the evening prior to say that he would take the morning train to Ninette and would spend the entire day with her. This made Lea very happy, and she was so anxious to see him.

"You will meet my husband today," Lea told Eva, as they ate their eggs and toast.

"It's always nice to get visitors," replied Eva.

"If he's coming by train, he won't be here until around lunchtime," noted Nurse Harriet. "Don't go getting your hopes up that he will be here for the entire day. If he returns by train, he'll have to leave by three as well."

There she was again, thought Lea—matter-of-fact Nurse Harriet. She even looked like a sergeant-major! She was very tall for a woman, likely almost six feet, a little husky and had long auburn hair that was always tight in a bun behind her nurse's cap.

Overall though, Lea enjoyed how everyone she had met at Ninette so far, staff and patients, were kind and friendly towards her. The staff seemed to really enjoy their work, and other patients were understanding and empathetic.

Just before lunch, she and her roommate conversed some more. She found out that Eva was from Brandon, a fairly large town northeast of Souris. Eva had been in Ninette for a long time, since she was fifteen, but she was confident that she would be going home soon. She had made great strides since her surgery last fall, when she had gone to the Central Tuberculosis Clinic in Winnipeg. They both found it peculiar that they had both been operated on the same day—October 17. Eva surmised that this would possibly now be their lucky day. Lea was not in the least the superstitious type, but she could see that a younger, more whimsical Eva was enjoying the coincidence of this, and to appease her, she played along.

"Yes, we'll have to see." Lea responded.

Lunch was once again a wonderful treat—macaroni and cheese, coleslaw, another slice of bread with butter, a glass of milk, and date pudding for dessert.

As soon as she finished her last bite, Louis walked in the door. He nodded briefly at the sight of Lea's new roommate and then went over to his wife's bedside and they embraced.

"This is quite the place" said Louis. "It's so big, yet so peaceful."

"It's wonderful here Louis," said Lea. "They do so much good. The doctors and nurses are all so efficient and professional. The surroundings are beautiful. The rooms are well-equipped with all kinds of extras. They feed us well. The place is everything it should be... except it's not home."

March 18, 1933

Cher Louis,

Just a few lines to let you know that I had x-rays taken on Monday after you left, and on Tuesday, two doctors came to examine me. On Wednesday, a third doctor came by to take a sample of the fluid in my wounds. I was told that they didn't think there was any tuberculosis in my wounds, but they did find holes in my intestines and would need to do further tests. I may possibly need another operation. Again last night, they told me there was no tuberculosis in my wounds and the holes in my intestines were so small, it was nothing really. So, I may be out of here quickly.

I am eating well. I drink milk at each meal, and at lunch time today, they gave me a big piece of butter, which I put on my potatoes.

That's all for today.

Lea, who thinks of you and my two little dear ones always

March 18, 1933

Chère Maman,

I received your letter. It was returned to Grande Clairière and then forwarded here. What luck! My dear Maman, there is no tuberculosis in my abdomen. This means I don't necessarily need to be here and could go anywhere I wanted if I don't get any better. Then again, there is no better place for me than here. They have all the amenities and it would be difficult to find a place that would treat me better.

Maman, could you wash my navy sweater and bring it with you when you come visit? The sweater I have here now doesn't tie at the neck, and the nurses have told me that I will be sleeping on the balconies here when the weather improves. Let me assure you that I

*am eating very well. The food is much differ-
ent than at Souris. What a nice surprise! I also
drink three cups of milk a day.*

*That's all for today. As always, many kisses to
my dear little ones.*

*Your daughter, who thinks of you often,
Lea*

As much as Sylvie hated that her daughter was so much further away from their home town, she realized that Lea was in the right place. Ninette Sanatorium was unrivalled in terms of patient care. Built in 1909, the facilities were exemplary, with such features as electric lighting throughout, indoor toilets, and modern medical equipment. The staff had a stellar reputation. Sylvie knew that if there was any one place that could find a cure for what was ailing Lea, it would be there.

Being so far away also meant that Sylvie would not likely be able to visit Lea as often. As it was, Sylvie had only visited in Souris a few times. Now, it would be near impossible. Stricter rules about children's visitation would also prevent Jean and Maurice from seeing their mother. Young children were simply not allowed to visit. As much as Sylvie knew that this would make her daughter very sad, she understood the rule. Heaven knows, no one would want them to be exposed to the tuberculosis bacteria that must certainly be lurking everywhere in those buildings.

Sylvie planned to visit Lea in the next month and wondered what she could bring her, besides her navy sweater that might brighten Lea's spirits. She thought of making some of her famous sucre à crème, and perhaps a bottle of her fortified wine.

She wondered if she should tell Lea what rumours were being spread in the village. Louis had apparently been spending much of his down time in the pool hall. He was never unruly or anything. But town folk were concerned that he was not taking care of himself. Visibly, one could see he had lost a lot of weight. Emotionally, he was withdrawn. He barely talked to anyone and spent most of his time staring into his glass. Lost. Lonely. Sylvie understood what was happening. She chose not to say anything to Lea, but thought perhaps she should try to talk to Louis and help him through this.

March 24, 1933

Cher Louis,

I've had three x-rays taken again this week. The last one was taken by the little man you met last week. I asked him if there was something serious going on with me, and he said no. I didn't ask the other technician when he came by, and he didn't tell me anything. Sometimes I am afraid that my intestines are damaged.

For the past three days, I've had horrible bouts of diarrhea.

They just took me for yet another x-ray. I'm not exactly sure what they did to me. They kept me there for over an hour and injected some type of fluid into my wounds. I don't believe that things are improving as they are now talking about possibly sending me to Winnipeg for an operation. It is odd that when I was in Souris, they never noticed that my intestines were full of holes. They should have known. The doctors here say that they have been this way for a long time.

I hope the little ones are doing well. That is all for today. I don't yet have the results of the tests they took.

As always, give kisses and hugs to my dear little ones... my poor little ones... will I ever see them again?

I send you my love from far away,
Lea

Chère Maman,

Two words to let you know that I'm feeling well enough, but I'm worried about my intestines. I'm quite sure that I may need another operation... and then who knows what will happen? There is no better place for me than here. The nurses are really good.

Jean must be proud of his new clothes. Is Maurice running around the house on all fours? Those poor little ones... will I ever have the chance to see them again?

When you come to see me, you will laugh at me and I'll warn you why in advance. My hair was falling in my eyes and becoming unmanageable, so the nurses asked if I would mind if they cut it. So now, I have the head of a child.

That's all for today. Kisses, as always, to Jean and Maurice for me.

Your daughter, who thinks of you often,
Lea

When Lea was a patient in Souris, she would have tests performed on her once a week, if that. Since she had been at Ninette Sanatorium, she'd had tests performed on her every day. If it wasn't an x-ray, it was a blood test or a urine sample. One particular procedure had her completely bloated with a white fluid that was injected into her abdomen. This test was called a fluoroscopy. Depending on what the test revealed, there was a chance that she could require surgery. She was told that should surgery be required, it could not be done at Ninette. She would have to be sent to one of the major hospitals in Winnipeg.

Lea could not fathom the idea of being moved again. She had just been moved from one facility to another. How could she possibly handle another move? And once again, she would be much further from home. Surely, no one would ever be able to visit her in Winnipeg. And would the operation be successful? Could she even survive it? Lea realized she needed to trust her doctors and do what they wanted her to do. They knew best. She decided to have faith in their abilities.

Being so far away from Grande Clairière, visitors were few and far between. Louis managed to get there twice the first week, once by train, and once with her brother, Georges. He cautioned that this would not always be possible and that she should just get used to the fact that they wouldn't be able to see each other as often. Friends and family weren't as keen to drive Louis all the way to Ninette. It took much too long, and most couldn't afford the gas for their vehicles as it was. Taking the train cost almost five dollars for a round trip ticket. Luckily for Louis, track maintenance work was ramping up a bit and he was beginning to get steady hours.

Ninette Sanatorium had a lot to offer however, and Lea was kept busy with many things. She spent most afternoons on the outside balcony. The weather was improving day-by-day. The sun made its appearance every day in March, and all traces of snow disappeared by the end of the month. The ice on the lake had begun to melt, bringing a new treat to the senses, the faint sound of water hitting the shore. Lea looked forward to the signs of the new season… buds on the trees, birds chirping, wildflowers springing up in the fields. On warmer days, she truly enjoyed being out on the balcony. It was restful to lie on her bed, with a light breeze flowing upon her face. Lea would breathe in the fresh air as deep in her chest as she could. This gave her a feeling of well-being that she hadn't had for a very long time.

Though the sanatorium emphasized the importance of rest, they also had limited, low-energy activities to keep the patients occupied and make the time pass by. Those patients who were able to sit up were allowed to play cards or board games. The healthier ones were sent to the main building for rehabilitation training and work. Almost daily, someone would come around with a cart full of books and magazines. Once in a while, Lea would grab something to read, but most days—between her morning treatments and tests, and her afternoons on the balcony—she ended returning items unread. If and when she did have enough energy, she chose to write letters.

Each day, for the most part, Lea would lay flat on her bed, not playing cards or games, not reading, not writing… only thoughts of Louis, Jean, Maurice, her mother and the rest of her family swirling in her head… and time went by ever so slowly.

March 29, 1933 was a particularly tough day. Lea woke up earlier than usual, knowing full well it was young

Jean's third birthday. She stayed awake and dwelled on it all day. Maman had not yet visited Lea in Ninette, but had managed to send a few letters, filling her in on how much the boys were growing and how well-behaved they were. For Jean's birthday, her mother had sewed him two pairs of pants. She'd also purchased a wooden toy truck for him at Hill's Store in Hartney and told Jean it was a special gift from his maman et papa.

March 30, 1933

Cher Louis,

I received your letter. I forgot to tell you the last time I wrote that, after all the examinations the doctors have given me, they have decided that I don't need another operation at this time. They take fluid samples from my wounds every two or three days, and tell me that they are always testing to ensure that I don't have tuberculosis. So far, they haven't found anything.

Every morning, the nurses wash my wounds and drain it using a tube. It is so painful when they do this. Sometimes, I think it would be less painful if they would cut me up in pieces. I suppose I have to suffer if I want to get better.

You tell me that you will come if you need to, but for now, I am fine. It might be best if you stay home, and use whatever money you have to buy the things you need. If you go a month without seeing me, however, you might not recognize me! They put me on the balcony every afternoon.

Yes, I would love to get a photo of Jean and Maurice. Our little Jean turned three yesterday. I thought of him all day. I thought of how happy we were when we were all together.

That's all for today.
Kisses to Jean and Maurice for me.

Lea, who loves you so much

Louis and Léon lifted the last of the boxes onto the truck borrowed from one of the residents of Grande Clairière. Just before leaving the vacated house, Louis took one quick look around to be sure he hadn't missed anything. As he walked from room to room, he realized he hadn't taken down the curtains Lea had sewn for each of the windows. He removed each of them, careful not to damage them, and as he did, he thought of how different the mood was when the curtains were going up.

Thinking he was going to surprise his wife, Louis had put them up at the crack of dawn one morning, only to find out that he hung them in the wrong rooms. Lea had laughed so much at him, wondering how he could think that the white see-through curtains belonged in the bedroom, and the dark blue linen ones belonged in the kitchen. They both laughed about it and Lea teased him about it for days. For a quick second, Louis smirked, and then realized the reality of what taking them down meant. Things were so different now.

Louis returned to the truck, dropped the pile of curtains in one of the boxes, set the curtain rods down, and hopped on the passenger side.

"Let's get out of here," he told his brother, and they headed over to Sylvie's house. Louis didn't dare look back.

Though most of their belongings were going to his mother-in-law's, Louis had decided that he would spend some time living at his own mother's house, just a few miles further. He didn't want to be a burden to Sylvie. Of course, both places were a good distance away from the train station, but spring was definitely in the air, so walking a few miles to the train station would not be an issue.

Louis had taken two days off without pay to move. He couldn't really afford it, but he had no choice. The house had been neglected for months and needed a lot of work before he handed it back to the municipality. Louis packed items and cleaned for two days straight from morning until night. He barely had time to make himself anything to eat, let alone go see Lea or visit with the children. He chose to stay overnight in the rented house while he could, and he drowned his sorrows with a bottle of whiskey.

The next day, it was only on the way to Sylvie's, with a truck full of his young family's belongings, that he realized he had missed his eldest son's birthday.

When Louis arrived at Sylvie's place, young Jean ran out to see his father, new truck in hand, and shouted loudly, "Merci, Papa." Louis looked up at Sylvie perplexed. She put her finger to her lips and smiled wryly.

"Our secret" she said as she helped unpack the boxes.

CHAPTER 8

April 1933

April 1, 1933

Chère Maman,

Just a few lines to let you know that things are always about the same. The nurses tell me that I am getting better, but I don't see it. Louis tells me that you may be able to visit me here with Bertha next week. I would be so happy to see you both! It's too bad it is so expensive to come here by train, but like you've always told me, "If you spend five dollars on a good deed, another $5 will find you." Please, don't bring me any jelly. I have some here, and they feed me so well that I really don't need anything else. I have nothing else to say for now. I hope to see you next week.

Hugs and kisses to my two dear little ones.
How sad that I am now so far away from them.
One day, hopefully, I will have the chance to be
near them again. But when?

Your daughter,
Lea

Lea was becoming quite accustomed to her new life at the sanatorium. She was kept fairly busy with routine matters, x-rays, tests and her daily trip to the balconies. She especially enjoyed being outside. The weather improved daily and she loved that the outside air was so fresh and clean. It also now had the aroma of early spring blossoms. Three times a day, she looked forward to the meals that were prepared for her, just to see what would be served next. She still marvelled at the difference in both quantity and quality of the food from when she was in Souris. Unfortunately, most of the time, she had little or no appetite, and couldn't take advantage of it.

Lea was also becoming better acquainted with her roommate and the other patients in Ninette. While on the balcony, she befriended other women. Some were mothers just like her, who had spent long periods of time away from their children. She took comfort in these new friendships. These women understood each other, many times with barely a word said.

Saturday soon became the day Lea anticipated the most. That was the day that Louis was most likely to visit. He would take the train, arriving just around lunchtime, and he was able to stay until just before three. And so, on this third Saturday since Lea had been there, Louis arrived just after twelve, as predicted. Lea was all smiles when she saw him. The same could not be said for Louis.

"You look so sad today," Lea remarked.

Louis just stared at her but said nothing. Lea felt she knew exactly what her husband might be thinking.

"You've had a difficult week Louis. I know. Giving up the house must have been terrible. And a lot of work. Did Léon help you?"

"Yes, I had help." After a long pause, he said "I am without a home to call my own now, Lea. I am homeless. A bum."

"Louis," Lea said sternly. "This was necessary. You know this. Don't go feeling sorry for yourself. Now is not the time to pity ourselves. We just have to take it day by day, and hopefully, before long, things will resolve themselves." As Lea spoke the words, she knew that she too needed to abide by them.

Louis changed the subject. "What happened to your hair? You look like a boy." He said it in a tone that was almost petulant and gruff.

Lea didn't appreciate his comment or his tone, but she thought it best not to react to it. "The nurses cut it. It was getting too long and difficult to wash. I like it this way. No fuss." As good as the nurses were, they sure weren't hair-dressers. And after they cut Lea's hair, which had grown well past her shoulders while in Souris, it was definitely short. She now had black strands that were only about an inch off her head, cut so that her ears now showed, and the back was barely past the nape of her neck. She now had bangs a few inches above her eyebrows. Lea knew her haircut wasn't exactly fashionable, but it was convenient, which is why she went along with it.

For the first time since she'd been sick, it suddenly occurred to Lea that her husband may not see her in a romantic light anymore. Had she been sick for too long? Had too much time passed since they'd been intimate?

"Am I still pretty to you, Louis?" said Lea, as she looked down at how thin she had become.

"Of course you are! Why would you say that?"

"I just don't feel pretty anymore. When I look into a mirror, I barely recognize myself. I think to myself, 'Who is that sickly person with the grey skin and sunken cheeks?' Do you see the same thing?"

"Lea," Louis said as he pulled her toward him. "Each time I look into your big blue eyes, I see the beautiful woman I fell in love with. Always. That will never change, ever."

They spent the rest of the day talking about other things, mostly the boys and how Jean was thoroughly enjoying the gifts he'd received for his birthday. They talked about her mother purchasing a new toy truck for Jean and telling him it was from Maman et Papa. Lea was not the least bit surprised by her mother's thoughtfulness.

"That is just what Maman would do! My, how I miss her!"

"She and Bertha are talking about coming here for a visit next week by train. Your nieces will look after the boys."

This bit of good news kept Lea in a good frame of mind for the remainder of Louis' visit. She missed her family so much. Since moving to Ninette, she'd barely had any visitors. Other than Louis, she'd only had one family visit, from her brother Georges. He had come with the great news that his only daughter was recently married.

Lea thought seeing her mother and sister would be a great distraction. She hoped she could see her sister Palmyre again, but she also knew this would not be possible. The baby was due in the next month. Lea wished she'd seen her sister pregnant. Normally, Palmyre was as thin as Lea, and just a tad shorter. Rumour had it that she had gained a lot of weight with this pregnancy—even on her arms, legs and face—and for the first time in her life, she actually looked pudgy. How Lea would have loved to have seen that!

"Tell Maman to bring in a photo of the children." Lea reminded Louis. "I so wish I could see them. I can only imagine how much they've grown by now."

By the time Louis left, he was in much better spirits than when he arrived. On the train ride home, he thought of how cunningly Lea could turn his thoughts to positive ones. She certainly had a way with words. Even after all this time away from each other, intuitively, they still knew how to guide each other through dark moments.

Maman and Bertha did come for a visit the following Friday, three days before Lea's twenty-ninth birthday. They walked in with a nicely gift-wrapped box and a round birthday cake, sitting atop a clear glass cake stand.

"How did you ever carry that on a train?" Lea laughed, as they walked through the door.

"We took turns" said Bertha. "We even had a few other passengers take their turn at holding the darn thing. It's surprising it isn't damaged, or half eaten!"

Lea had a pleasant visit with her mother and sister, though she found Maman was rather quiet. Bertha did most of the talking, keeping Lea abreast with family and town news, who was getting married, who had had a baby, who was sick, and who had died. The family was looking forward to the arrival of Léon and Palmyre's new baby.

Lea opened the gift and was delighted to see a framed photograph of Jean and Maurice. Maman explained that she had taken it just before Christmas, but had not had the chance to develop the film until last month. She'd found a frame for the photo at Hill's Store in Hartney.

"Look at them," sighed Lea. "They are so grown up, so handsome. My boys are so handsome!" She wiped tears from her eyes as she gazed at the black and white photograph. "Do they still look like this now?"

"Yes, of course," Bertha reassured her. "They are both very nice looking and well-behaved."

"Maurice has changed a bit" Maman added. "He is able to stand up by himself now, but hasn't dared to take a step alone yet."

Lea held onto the frame the entire time her mother and sister were there, and stared at it constantly. How she longed to see her dear little ones again. She so wanted to hold them in her arms and rock them to sleep. At least now, she had a photo of them, albeit one taken four months ago.

All told, Lea had a delightful visit with her mother and sister. They ate cake, sharing some with her roommate Eva and the nurses on duty. They even gave a piece to the lady who came by with the books and magazines. Lea made mention that this cake should also represent a celebration of Maman's birthday, which was just five days after Lea's. About to turn sixty-nine years old, Sylvie scoffed at any attempt to celebrate. "After this many years, celebrating birthdays doesn't seem as important" said Sylvie. "It's just another day."

Lea remained in good spirits until April tenth, the day of her actual birthday. On that day, a Monday, not one of her family members was able to visit, not even Louis. By the end of the day, Lea was sad and dejected. In all the time she had been away, she'd never felt more alone than on that particular day. She tried to change her thoughts by repeating to herself what her mother had told her just a few days ago, "It's just another day."

Though Lea was told by the medical staff that she was improving, she did not feel she was getting better. Physically, she still felt weak and infected. Deep down in her heart, she knew that she wasn't well. Months of being in bed was also starting to take its emotional toll. Lea found it so difficult to keep thinking positively. At times, she also found it challenging to think clearly. It had been months since she'd read a book, or even an article in a newspaper or magazine, and she didn't even have the urge to do so. This was so unlike her. Slowly but surely, Lea felt like she was fading.

April 12, 1933
Cher Louis,

Not much has changed since you were last here. Pus continues to leak from my wounds every day, although it seems to be less than before. The doctor visits me daily, but never comments on my condition. The nurses all seem to think that my abscess is much improved from when I first arrived here. It has been a month now since I've been here. I wish I knew how many more days I need to be here yet. Kisses to Jean and Maurice, my two poor little ones. I wish I knew if I will ever see them again.

Lea, who thinks of all of you all the time

The doctors at Ninette met on a regular basis to discuss the patients in their care. In the month since Lea Mahy had been admitted, her particular case had been discussed extensively.

Six months after Mrs. Mahy's surgery, her stomach was still distended and pus continued to flow from two wounds on either side of her appendectomy incision. Based on the severity of the infection, the doctors thought that the patient may benefit from the re-opening of the surgical incision site to allow wound drainage. To achieve this, however, the patient would have to be sent to a health facility in Winnipeg. Ninette was meant for medical management of tuberculosis diseases and did not have any operating facilities. The doctors worried that the drive alone could jeopardize the frail young woman's health. They were also concerned that she may not be able to tolerate a second surgery.

In the month since she'd been at Ninette, the patient had adapted well to her new environment and the outdoor rest seemed to be helping her both physically and emotionally. The wound discharge seemed to be decreasing slightly, though not as much as they'd hoped. Due to the doubts about the patient's tolerability of this second operation, the decision was to withhold it until the patient was more medically fit.

April 19, 1933

Cher Louis,

A word to give you some news, which is always about the same. One wound is barely leaking anymore and it almost looks as though it is slowly closing up. The other wound, on the other hand, has been causing me a lot of pain for the last few days. I don't think this is anything to worry about though.

As of last Sunday, I have been on my back for six full months. Let me tell you... time goes by very slowly. And how much longer will I need to be here? If only I could see my boys. It has been four months since I last saw Jean and three months since I last saw Maurice. I miss them so much. If we at least knew that eventually things will be better... I'm afraid this may not ever be the case.

That's all for today. Don't forget to give hugs to my dear little ones.

Lea, who thinks of you always

Ever since Louis had vacated the house, he spent most of his spare time at his mother's, four miles up the road from Sylvie's house. He spent most every weekday working. He was one of the lucky ones who had kept

his job during the depression, and he was now working three to five days a week. The days were long as he had to take an early train from Grande Clairière each morning to his work site. In the evening, he would usually hitch a ride back with someone. He would then walk over to see the boys at Sylvie's for about an hour each evening, before they went to bed. By then, Sylvie was usually tired and ready for bed herself, so he would head over to his mother's and stay there for the night.

This was a temporary arrangement however, as Marie Mahy also had to move by the end of April. Many years earlier, she had sold her house and surrounding land, but was able to stay in her home and rent it from the buyer with the proceeds. Now, this money was depleted and she could no longer afford to stay there at all. Her good friend Rosalie Delaite offered her a room in her home right in town, and this bode well for the elderly woman, as she would then live just across the street from the church, where she could go daily and pray for better days.

Marie Mahy's house was a small, well-kept one-storey, filled only with very basic pieces of furniture, and ornately decorated with many religious artifacts. The walls were adorned with framed prints of Jesus, the Virgin Mary, and one of Pope Pius XI. Crosses were placed above each doorway. A gold-framed lithograph of the Last Supper hung above her dining table. When Louis sat in his mother's home and looked around at all these religious items, he couldn't help but wonder how his mother's dedication to Catholicism had helped, or failed to help, his family. Despite her prayers and devotion to God, the Mahy family still endured many tragedies. He lost his father, a brother, and two sisters well before their time. And now, he felt as though he was losing his wife.

Louis and his mother rarely said much to each other during those evenings. If and when they did talk to each other, it was small talk. How was Lea? How were the boys? How was Sylvie handling the extra load of caring for them? Never did they discuss his gut-wrenching feelings of hopelessness or despair. That would only lead to a discussion about faith and religion, and Louis just couldn't bring himself to tell his mother what he really felt on the subject. Instead, he appeased her when she asked him to gather by the votives each evening to ask God for healing and forgiveness. He accompanied her to Easter Sunday mass and he pretended to pray each night. Some things were better left unsaid.

Each Saturday, Louis would take the train to Ninette to visit Lea. He had found her spirits wavering of late, and knew she needed regular visits from him. Despite the fact that both of them were feeling deflated, they managed to find things to talk about, and still talked often about the possibilities in the future. However small, they clung on to the hope that eventually, things would improve.

On Sundays, Louis would try to spend time with his boys. Sometimes, he would take Jean for a buggy ride into town or to visit his relatives in surrounding areas. Other times, he walked to town with both boys, or just played in the yard. His mother tried to encourage him to start taking the boys to church each Sunday, but Louis knew all too well that doing so would entail a lot of work just trying to keep the boys quiet.

April 19, 1933

Chère maman,

You must be happy to receive my letters.

Unfortunately, there is no news to tell you. Not much has changed. There is still quite a bit of discharge coming from my incision.

Have you eaten the beans and the cauliflower? Let me know if they are still good after all this time. If they are, eat them as it's very unlikely that I will ever be home in time to eat them.

I am losing hope, my dear mother, though I do feel a little stronger than before. My temperature has been high lately, but I am eating well. There is such a big difference in food quality here compared to Souris. It's still not as good as home cooking however. If I was home, I would eat even better. But, I am here and this is where I must stay for now.

It has been six months, dear mother, since I've been on my back. How much longer will I have to stay here? If only I knew that one day I would be healed and could return home to my dear little "lou-lou's," as Jean used to say to me. I must stop writing… my eyes are filled with tears.

I received a big box of chocolates from Eaton's for Easter. Were these from you? If so, thank you so much.

Kisses to all of you.
Lea

Truth be told, Sylvie rarely felt 'happy' when she received letters from Lea. They were a reminder of the suffering her daughter had to bear each day. They always gave grim details of Lea's less than optimistic condition. Mostly, they oozed heart-wrenching words, constantly bemoaning how much she missed her sons.

Tired and busy as she was, Sylvie knew that she had to do something to bring her daughter's spirits up. The day after receiving Lea's letter, Sylvie took out her camera. She knew she was near the end of the film roll, as she had taken photos recently at two weddings. She could get the roll sent to Winnipeg to be developed right away. She had two photographs left, so she decided that she would take individual shots of the boys.

Outside, it was sunny and warm. The snow had all melted and there was no wind. This would be a perfect day to walk over to the general store with the boys. She could pull the baby in the toy wagon and young Jean would walk beside her.

She put light sweaters on each of them and headed outside, thinking that would be the best place to take photographs. She placed Maurice in the wagon and tried to snap a photo of him in that window of time when he looked at his surroundings, before he tried to leap out of the wagon. Next, she had Jean stand in the shade of an oak tree, still bare of leaves, and pressed on the shutter button. It was hard to tell how the photos would turn out, but whatever expression the boys had on their faces, Lea would be happy to see them.

Sylvie enjoyed the walk to the general store. Jean was so happy to be outside on such a nice spring day that he skipped and played all the way down the road. Maurice was equally excited just sitting in the wagon and taking in the sights as Grandmaman pulled him along. Once she arrived in town, she met up with friends and neighbours, who marvelled at how much the boys had grown over the winter. Yes, she thought, and soon their mother would see how much they had grown as well, if only on a piece of Kodak paper.

April 27, 1933

Ma chère Lea,

I take pencil in hand to let you know that the beans you canned last fall were delicious. We ate the whole jar last Saturday for supper.

I am sending you photos of the children. They didn't turn out very well. We will take some better ones for you at a later date.

I haven't planted my garden yet. I am hoping to plant some onions and carrots soon, and maybe a bit of cabbage for now. If things go well for you, we will share these.

I can see that you are doing well. Continue to be strong. I have great hopes for you.

Your mother,
Sylvie Charles

On a warm but foggy morning on the last day of April, Lea had just settled in on the balcony. She brought along a letter that she had just received from her mother.

Upon opening the envelope dated April twenty-ninth, she could feel that there was something thicker than just a piece of paper inside. To her great surprise and pleasure, she found two photos of her boys.

The first one was of baby Maurice, sitting in an old wooden wagon that Lea had also sat in when she was a child. He looked as though he was just about to climb out of it, and the photo was quite blurry as a result. Lea laughed out loud! She thought back to when Jean was that age and he was so squirmy she could barely change his diaper without him bouncing all around the bed. No doubt, Maurice had that same energy. What Lea could make out was that her youngest child had changed so much since she'd last seen him. He was definitely taller and seemed to have slimmed down some, though he still had his chubby cheeks. She could see that he was sturdy enough to sit and stand up on his own. This saddened her somewhat, because it reminded her of all the precious milestones of his that she had missed.

Jean too looked taller and more grown up. He was standing beside a tree, but clearly not at the right spot, as no amount of shade was covering his face. His head was down somewhat and his eyes were squinted, but he was looking directly at the camera lens. This photograph was a little clearer, and Lea noticed immediately that Jean looked sad. His eyes looked sad. And they were staring right at her. The moment Lea looked into Jean's eyes, she felt a breeze across her face and body, enough to make her shiver. Somehow, she felt enveloped in love. It was as though her son's eyes pierced through the paper and touched her heart.

Lea unfolded her mother's letter and read it. And then read it again. She was astonished, not so much about what her mother had written, but what she didn't write. She found it odd that her mother took the time to go into detail about what she wanted to plant in her garden, yet she didn't mention a word about how the boys were, or any news about them. And then there was the line "I can see that you are doing well." Lea couldn't understand how her mother could interpret from her previous letters and visits that she was "doing well." For a moment, Lea thought that perhaps her mother was not feeling well herself. Certainly, she didn't seem to be in touch with her feelings the way she usually was. Lea would ask Louis about her on his next visit.

Throughout the day, Lea would put the photographs down and then pick them up again. Each time she looked at Jean's picture, she would get the same feeling. Jean's piercing eyes were looking directly at her, as though he was communicating with her.

Lea read her mother's letter again. Taken aback by her mother's words, she decided that her next letter to her mother would include more sordid details about the reality of her situation.

CHAPTER 9
May 1933

May 3, 1933

Cher Louis et chère maman,

I will write but one letter to you both, because I always repeat the same thing to each of you. I received the photos of the boys. Jean looks so grown up and I can see that Maurice is still a big baby. My dear little ones... will I ever again have the pleasure of seeing them? When I look at Jean, it seems as though he is speaking to me. My dear mother, this is all so difficult. Some days I have hope, but other days I am very discouraged... so much so, that, for a long time now, I have wished that I would cross over to the other world.

For the last few days, I have had a lot of discharge from the incision. The nurses continue to wash this away daily and this makes me suffer, but the pain doesn't last too long. If only this little wound would heal.

Do you think either of you will be able to visit me soon? I know it isn't easy for either of you to come here… Maybe ask Emile if he would bring you this Sunday.

I've been drinking milk every day, but I can't get used to the taste. In fact, it disgusts me.

That's all for today.
Lea, who misses you always

Writing was becoming a chore for Lea. What once gave her such pleasure was now a monumental task. This upset her to no end, but she was wise enough to understand that her illness was taking away her will to write, and that once she regained her health, she would want to write again.

So what was at the root of this feeling of great malaise? Yes, weakness from such prolonged time in a bed played a large part, but Lea knew that wasn't the only issue. Lately, she noticed that, in addition to feeling constantly fatigued, she often felt dizzy and nauseous. She speculated that she was possibly being given medications that were perhaps too potent for her. At times, she avoided writing because she found it hard to put sentences together, or keep her thoughts straight. Louis had even mentioned the last time he visited that he wasn't sure what she had meant at a certain point in her last letter. This was not at all like Lea. She usually wrote with such clarity.

Luckily, family and friends continued to write to her, and for this, Lea felt very blessed. In one week, she received mail from her mother, her mother-in-law, three of her sisters, Mme. Gauvreau, and her friend Nora. She loved receiving news from all these people whom she held so dear, and reading these letters over and over again did help to pass the time. She had not received a letter from Louis, but continued to see him every Saturday. She hoped that her brother Emile, who was still a bachelor, would have the time to take Maman and Louis all the way to Ninette now that he had a vehicle.

Medically, yet another issue had arisen. Lea began to have regular bouts of diarrhea. She'd had occasional occurrences in Souris, but since she had been at Ninette, it happened with much more frequency. She wondered if the milk she was drinking there had anything to do with it. She found the taste of the milk in Ninette so fowl, not at all like milk from home. Perhaps this was upsetting her stomach and her intestines. The medical personnel at Ninette were not at all convinced though, and encouraged Lea to continue to drink it. They were aware of her intestinal issues however, and were watching her closely.

May 10, 1933
Cher Louis,

It has been awhile since I've received news from you, but I know that you are probably too busy to write. As for news from here, I am feeling well enough but am still having continued intestinal issues. In spite of this, I am eating well. The incision scar is still about the same. The nurses tell me that it is not nearly as infected as it used to be, but I still see a lot of pus coming out of there.

Did you do anything for Lent? I received a letter from your mother and that is pretty much all she talked about... that you are not going to church much and that you didn't pray more or fast during lent. You might as well listen to her.

The doctor always asks me about my outside wound when he comes to see me, but he rarely mentions what is going on internally. I'm guessing he doesn't want to tell me where things stand, because he knows that I am afraid of getting another operation. In the end, I know that if being operated is the only option, I will do it. My only hesitation is that it keeps me away from my two babies that much longer, even though I know they are in good hands.

Lea, who thinks only of you and the boys

May 10, 1933

Chère Maman,

I received your letter this morning. You tell me to always be strong. Yes, chère maman, it's all that I can do. But you must know that it is not always easy. It has been nearly seven months since I have been flat on my back. My strength is coming back ever so slowly. I have been getting severe intestinal pains lately, and this is preventing me from sitting up.

You tell me that you would like to come to see me. I suppose you could come by train during the week, as long as you have someone to look after Jean and Maurice. If you can have someone give you a ride here on a Sunday, Louis could look after the boys.

Supper has just arrived. I wonder what they have in store for me today. Though the food is good here, I would prefer to be home and eat to my taste. Most mornings, I have porridge and toast. Just once, I wish I could have some re-heated potatoes. I just need to be more patient, I suppose.

That is all for today. Give hugs and kisses to Jean and Maurice for me, my dear little ones.

Lea, your daughter who loves you.

The very morning that Sylvie received Lea's latest letter, she had thought of taking a train to Ninette to see her daughter. Her granddaughter Marguerite was helping her to look after the boys, and by now the young girl was quite accustomed to having both of them in her care at the same time. Sylvie knew that Jean and Maurice would be in good hands, and that Lea would be thrilled if she went to visit her. It was a balmy, sunshiny day, a perfect day for travelling, but something wasn't quite right.

A few days prior, Sylvie had been asked by her daughter Roseanna to assist in delivering the latest baby in the family, a second daughter born to Palmyre and Léon. Sylvie was unable to help. She was too exhausted to simply walk down the road to their home, let alone help with the delivery. And from that point on, she just hadn't been able to get her energy level back up.

She still suffered from a pain in her groin, which she attributed to carrying little Maurice so much. She thought that perhaps she should call Dr. Riddell and get a check-up. But then again, it was likely just fatigue and a pulled groin muscle.

Every day in May was a blessing when it came to the weather. It was sunny most days, and warm, in the mid to high sixties. This boded well for Sylvie, who spent most of her days outside, often with the two little tykes at her side.

Young Jean loved being outside and spent much of his time running through the yard, swinging on a board and some rope hung from a tree or picking dandelions. The baby, who was now almost one, would sit on a blanket and play with whatever curious items his grandmother placed in front of him, be it a small pail, a gardening shovel, or a washboard. Once in a while, he would catch a glimpse of his big brother scampering around the yard and tried to join him, although all he could manage was a slow crawl.

Meanwhile, Sylvie tried to clean the weeds from the garden and prepare it for this year's crop. She'd had one of her sons till the land in preparation for seeding, but she took on the responsibility to hoe the rows herself, because she wanted them a certain width apart. Each day, she would plant three or four rows of vegetables. She hoped to have the garden completely planted by the end of May.

While she worked away outside at a slow pace, Sylvie fretted about whether Lea would ever recover from her illness. She had been away so long. Now that she was at Ninette…. Sylvie knew many families who had been impacted by tuberculosis, and those who were placed in the sanatorium's care usually stayed for a very long time. Even though Sylvie knew that Lea had not actually been diagnosed with tuberculosis, she still worried about her daughter's exposure to the other patients. Could her already-weakened immune system resist the contagious illness surrounding her?

As the days in May went by, Sylvie found it more and more difficult to visit Lea. In fact, by mid-month, she was feeling so unwell that she asked for additional help with the little ones. By the third week, arrangements were made for the boys to be cared for fully by others in the family. Little Jean was taken in temporarily by Bertha, and Roseanna took on the care of baby Maurice.

Sylvie remained at home. Members of her family stayed by her side at all times. They could all see that she was in a lot of discomfort. She slept on the living room couch for two days, unable to reach her bedroom on the second level. She had a fever and a bulging groin. She held her hand on her heart constantly and eventually found herself doubled over in pain. Finally, realizing that she was seriously ill, she asked one of her sons to go to Hartney to get Dr. Riddell.

By the time the good doctor arrived, it was too late. As he peered through the door's small window, he could see that she was lying completely still and her face was ashen. When he got in to examine her, he could see that her stomach was bulging and her breathing was shallow. She barely had a pulse, her heart rate was extremely low, and her blood pressure was not recordable. Dr. Riddell tried to resuscitate her with the hope of sending her to Souris Hospital for care. He soon realized that it was too late for that. Sylvie Charles was beyond help.

On the evening of May 23, 1933, the day of baby Maurice's first birthday, Sylvie Charles died of a strangulated hernia and acute intestinal obstruction. She was sixty-nine years old.

That very evening, Sylvie Charles' children made their way to their childhood home. There, they gathered to make funeral arrangements, clean out some of their mother's belongings, and make temporary arrangements for the care of Lea's boys. Outside, the skies were dark gray, the wind howled and rain poured down. To the family, it was as though the heavens were crying.

Sylvie's funeral was held three days later at St. Jean's Church in Grande Clairière. All members of her large family—her sons, daughters, sons-in-law, daughters-in-law, and grandchildren—attended, except for Lea. In fact, no one had dared tell Lea what tragedy had befallen the family. Louis knew only too well that this horrible news would only make Lea sink deeper. It would be over a week after her mother's death before Lea was ever told.

CHAPTER 10

June 1933

On the morning of the first day of June, Louis, Bertha, Roseanna, and Emile piled into Father Bertrand's Essex and drove out to the Ninette Sanatorium. Palmyre had wanted to be there so badly, but she also knew that it would not be wise, given that she had a newborn at home who needed her.

In the past two weeks, Lea had written letters to her husband and a few of her siblings, asking if any of them could visit her. She also asked how Maman was feeling. In his last visit, Louis had said that the pain in her side was still bothering her. That particular visit was on the Saturday before Sylvie died.

The following Saturday, four days after Sylvie died and two days after her funeral, Louis needed to spend time with his two young boys, who were still technically still living at Sylvie's house. Even more pressing, he needed to meet with members of the Charles family to discuss more permanent arrangements for the children. He sent a message to Lea's nurses, through the sanatorium telephone operator, that he would not be able to visit, but that he would make his way there in a few days. This, he thought, would buy him some time.

The ride to Ninette seemed longer than normal. Even though they left fairly early in the morning, the sun was already quite intense and shone directly into the front of the car as they drove east. It was easy to determine that the day would be hot and humid, and the inside of the vehicle would be unbearably warm.

Everyone in the car was pensive and the overall mood was sombre. They knew only too well that the task ahead of them would be difficult. As they drove onto the sanatorium grounds, each of Lea's siblings braced themselves for what was about to take place. Maman had always been such a huge part of young Lea's life. She was her mentor, her rock… a part of her soul. And now, she was gone.

As they stepped out of the car and headed toward the women's pavilion, Mendelssohn's *Songs without Words* played softly on the sanatorium's public address system. Maman had this recording at home and played it regularly, especially when she wanted some peaceful time. How uncanny that this beautiful piece of music would be playing at this exact moment.

Bertha looked up to the balconies, wondering aloud if Lea was already outside and whether she could see them. Louis told everyone that when he had called the sanatorium, he had alerted her nurse of what had happened and asked that Lea be kept in her room so that they would have some privacy to talk to her. They slowly walked up the steps at the back of the building to the third floor and headed toward Lea's room. Each of them hesitated and took a deep breath before entering.

"Mais qu'est-ce qui çe passe? What's happening?" Lea said when she saw all of them walk in. The look on her face revealed immediately that she knew something was wrong.

"C'est maman," started Roseanna, the eldest of Sylvie's daughters. She sat on the bed, took hold of Lea's frail hands and said, "We have some very bad news Lea." She paused for a moment, took a deep breath and then finally said "Maman died, Lea. She was very sick this last week. She had an obstruction, and by the time the doctor saw her, it was too late. There was nothing he could do to save her."

Lea sat motionless for a moment and then muttered, "That can't be. Mon Dieu! That mustn't be."

Thousands of thoughts cluttered Lea's mind. Her mother was gone. How could that happen so quickly? Her dear, sweet mother... who never complained about anything... who always put others before herself... the boys! Where were the boys? What would happen to the boys? Before she could express any of these thoughts outwardly, she broke down in tears and one by one, she was comforted by her husband and siblings.

"This can't be," was all that Lea could say.

Lea's siblings returned to Grande Clairière just before lunchtime. Before leaving, they all gathered around Lea's bed, and Father Bertrand led them in prayer. The parish priest blessed them all, asking God to give them strength in this time of sorrow. He then led them in reciting the rosary. Lea held her pink glass beads close to her heart, tears rolling down her cheeks.

Louis remained with Lea a few hours longer and took the late afternoon train back home. Lea was distraught at the fact that she had lost her mother, but she was also restless and anxious about what her mother's death would mean to her little family nucleus. As it was, the boys were no longer under the same roof. It would only be a matter of time before Louis would have to move out of Maman's house, too. Where would he live now?

They tried to talk things out and come up with some options, but both were too upset to come up with anything very well thought out. Instead, Louis spent most of the day lying beside his darling wife, holding her frail body in his arms and whispering whatever comforting words he could think of, as Lea wept and eventually fell asleep.

The remainder of the month did not go well for Lea. Physically, her body was deteriorating. Her symptoms only exacerbated once she heard of her mother's death. It was as though she had lost her will to live. Emotionally, she was drained. Coping with the loss of her mother, worrying about who would care for her sons... all this pressure was taking its toll.

She received many visits from her siblings during the month of June. Typically, conversations shifted to who would care for Jean and Maurice, at least for the time being. Palmyre had offered to take both boys, but having just had a baby a few weeks before her mother's passing, she was in no position to take on the responsibility of caring for two additional children. Most of Lea's other sisters also had very young children, one had a child on the way, and all were facing tough financial times. For most of them, feeding and raising their own family was trying enough.

A decision was made in the matter of little Maurice's care. Roseanna offered to care for him until Lea was back in Grande Clairière. She and her husband René would take him back to their farm and Louis could go visit him whenever he could find the time. As much as Louis hated that he could not look after his own flesh and blood, he knew that he had no choice. He was still working for the railway part time, and between work and visiting Lea, he could not take on the responsibility of caring for a one year old. Jean on the other hand... Louis was confident

that he could care for him with the help of both the Mahy
and Charles families.

Whenever Louis visited Lea, they talked about the
arrangements for the boys and whether they had done
the right thing by splitting the boys up. Both young
ones seemed to be quite adaptable. Maurice had not
reacted at all to being in a new home. If anything, he
seemed positively settled once his crib was brought to
the Hardy farm. If he missed his older brother, he didn't
show it. Jean on the other hand, was old enough to know
that much of his young life had changed. Where was
Grandmaman? When would he ever see Maman again?
Jean would spend three or four days a week with his
father. The rest of the time, he would either be at Uncle
Léon and Aunty Palmyre's, or with another one of his
many relatives. For the time being, both Louis and Jean
were staying in Sylvie's house. They knew however, that
this was a temporary arrangement, as the Charles family
worked on settling Sylvie's estate.

By the second week of June, medical staff at Ninette
Sanatorium could no longer put off the inevitable. Lea
would need an operation to drain the pus and fix the
holes on her intestines. A decision was made to have
the patient moved to the Central Tuberculosis Clinic
in Winnipeg, so that the operation could be performed there.

On June 15, 1933, an ambulance from Winnipeg
drove to Ninette to pick up Lea. Louis accompanied her.

As they left the grounds of the sanatorium, lively music played over public address system, and workers were tending to the grounds and preparing for the annual picnic, which was to occur in a few weeks' time. There was also a lot of talk about former Prime Minister McKenzie King visiting the sanatorium in July. Everyone was buzzing with the excitement of it all. Lea was too ill to participate in, or enjoy, any of the hoopla, and was too distraught to even want to try.

The operation did not go well. She barely survived it. The surgery also revealed that she did indeed have intestinal tuberculosis.

Louis stayed three full weeks in Winnipeg, bunking in overnight with the same friends Lea and Sylvie had stayed with four years prior, in Saint-Boniface and spending most of his days at his wife's bedside. These days were gruelling for him. Most of the time, Lea was unconscious. Often during those days, Louis fretted that he would never hear his wife speak again. Most of the time, he would just stare at her. Once in a while, he would whisper in her ear.

"Lea, if I would have known that one day I would be seeing you like this, I would have told you so much more how much you mean to me, how much I love you."

It would be five days after the operation before Lea would even open her eyes. When she finally did, she was so groggy and felt so ill, she just closed them again and turned away. For Louis, seeing her in this state—glossy eyes staring into space—was even harsher to see than when she was sleeping. Slowly, Louis was seeing his wife slip away.

"Talk to me, Lea. Give me a sign that you are trying to regain your life. Our story can't end here. Not like this."

CHAPTER 11

Summer 1933

By early July, Lea was beginning to gain some strength. She began to speak again, but in a soft, weakened tone. Most times, she didn't have very much to say. Almost always, she would ask about Jean and Maurice. At one point, she told Louis it was time for him to go back home to Grande Clairière. As much as Louis wanted to stay by his wife's side, he knew she was right. He had to go back to see his boys and back to work, if there was still work available for him.

Louis made arrangements for two of Lea's brothers to come to Winnipeg by automobile to pick him up. They would drive up early in the morning—a four or five hour trip—visit briefly with their sister, and return home with Louis the same day.

The day Louis left Lea's bedside was one of the toughest days he'd ever experienced. He stopped in for an early morning visit before heading out, and intended to stay until early afternoon, when Lea's brothers would arrive. When the time came, he couldn't leave her side. Lea was despondent most of the day. Louis spoke to the doctors at the CTC facility about when she could return to Ninette, but he was not given any indication that his wife would be able to leave the facility anytime soon. She was still much too ill. Louis convinced her brothers to delay the trip back by a few more hours, and stayed by his wife's side until just before six that evening, when they absolutely had to leave if they had any chance at all of making it back to Grande Clairière before dark.

Even as he kissed his wife on her forehead before leaving, she cringed as though any touch at all was painful. On the long car ride home, Louis admitted for the first time in this whole ordeal that he might need to prepare for life without her. Hope was fading.

July 10, 1933

Chère Lea,

I am writing you a few words to give you a bit of news. We got back OK. We arrived home at two o'clock in the morning. I quickly moved our stuff and that of our boys out of the house. Jean is living at Léon's for the time being. I will leave him there for now. Maurice has started walking.

Father Pierquin's father was buried in Grande Clairière cemetery at five o'clock today. I went to the service.

I have not much else to tell you.

You must not get discouraged Lea. If somehow you were able to return to us in a few months, the little ones and I would be so happy. We just have to hope that you will heal, or at least return to Ninette, where we could go spend every Sunday with you.

That is all for today.

Louis, who sends you hugs and loves you

The summer of 1933 was not an easy one for most of the residents of Grande Clairière. Drought and depression continued to batter the population. Many families moved away, due to unemployment and desperate times. Death took away many special people in the area, including the former parish priest's father, Mr. Paul Pierquin. Years earlier, Mr. Pierquin had started the first bank in Grande Clairière—the Banque de Hochelega, later renamed the National Bank. It was quite an accomplishment, and having a bank in town really helped to put Grande Clairière on the map.

For Louis, the harshness of how life could be stared him right in the face. He was without a home, his children were living miles apart in two different homes and his wife was even further away in a hospital in Winnipeg.

And as far as he could tell, Lea was not recovering from her illness.

Louis' mother and siblings were also finding these lean years tough to take, and every one of them were forced to make major decisions regarding how to continue to survive with little or no money. Marie Mahy moved in with friends; Léon struggled to find work in Grande Clairière, and he had the extra expenses of the new baby and little Jean; other siblings were scrambling just to make ends meet.

Ironically, when it came to work, Louis was one of the lucky ones. He still had a job. Once he returned from Winnipeg, he spent two or three days a week working on track maintenance. Often when he worked, he stayed on the road overnight. Then, on days off, he would return to Grande Clairière, stay at Léon's where he would see young Jean, and try to get out to visit with little Maurice when he could.

Though try as he might, Louis was just unable to get back to Winnipeg to visit Lea. The train schedule did not coincide with the times he was able to go. The cost of going by car and paying someone for gas was just too much. So was the time it took to get there. The little money Louis made was needed to buy food and basic necessities for him and his children, and arrear payments to Souris Hospital. Times were tough. The reality of life was tougher.

August, 1933 (postmarked Winnipeg)

Cher Louis,

Just a word to let you know that I have not been well the last few days. The issue with my wounds has started up again and let me tell you, there is a lot of discharge. Let's hope that things get better soon. I had a visit from the Souris police today. They had me sign the papers to confirm who I wanted to act as Executor on my behalf. I don't know if I did the right thing. That's all for now, as I am feeling very weak. Don't worry about it though. The doctor says that this is common. As always, kisses and hugs to the little ones.

Lea, who loves you very much

In mid-August, the CTC in Winnipeg decided it would be best if Lea was sent back to the Ninette Sanatorium. The prognosis was not good and there was a risk in moving her so far away, but the doctors at the clinic knew that she would be more comfortable, have more specialized care, and be nearer to family on the hallowed grounds of Ninette.

Just before leaving the Winnipeg clinic, Lea received a visit from police officers from Souris, who had some documents for her to sign. These papers gave a family acquaintance permission to act on Lea's behalf regarding any items related to her mother's estate. This was done to protect Louis, Jean and Maurice. Lea wanted to ensure that if anything should happen to her while her mother' estate was still unresolved, her entitlement would then be transferred to her husband and eventually, to her sons. Lea was very weak the day these men came. She was glad to see them though, because she knew the papers had to be signed to assure that her boys would get what rightfully belonged to them.

On August 23, she was returned to the sanatorium by ambulance and placed in the critical care infirmary in the main administration building. Visitors would be prohibited, aside from her husband, and even his visits would be kept to a minimum. Lea needed absolute rest.

She did have one very special visit in early September. Though leaves were starting to fall from the trees and the air was pungent with the traditional smells of autumn, it was as hot as a mid-summer day. It was a perfect day to travel with a toddler, so Louis set out by car, which he borrowed from a relative, and brought along young Jean. On the way, he explained to his son that his mother was very sick and that he would probably not see her for a long time after this visit. Nonetheless, the boy was thrilled to be given the chance to see her once again.

Lea knew full well that her prognosis was not good. But she also knew that Jean was still asking to see her. On Louis' last visit, she asked him to find a way to bring him. It would be good for both of them to see each other again.

As they stepped out of the car outside the administration building, young Jean began to sprint across the road. Louis hollered at him to stop. Inevitably, the child was anxious.

Louis took hold of Jean's hand and walked with him towards the doorway. Before entering, he reiterated how ill Maman was and that he would have to behave nicely and be very quiet once they were inside. Once they arrived, Lea's nurse was called to meet them just inside the entrance.

"Come with me," she said to Louis. "I will bring you to your wife's room. I believe that she is sleeping right now, but she has asked specifically that I wake her up when you get here. You must keep this visit very short."

When they entered the room, there was no need to wake Lea up. She was already awake and had her pillows propped so that she was semi-sitting on her bed. She had already made room for Jean to sit right beside her.

Young Jean didn't know what to say. Nor did he know if he should be happy or sad. He immediately recognized his mother's eyes and smile, but he barely knew her voice. This voice was softer, gravelly. He was a little frightened by how frail she was and how sick she appeared to be. He stared at her and said nothing.

Lea could barely speak herself. She asked him if he had been a good boy. She asked him if he liked living at his cousin Aurélie's house. She told him how grown up he looked and how proud she was of him. She told him that she loved him very much. She drew him nearer to her and stroked his light brown hair and his soft, rosy cheeks.

The boy leaned on her extended arm and patted her shoulder. Louis could only stand at the doorway and admire the love between his wife and his eldest son.

The visit was no more than thirty minutes. Very few words were uttered, but to Lea and Louis, all was very clearly understood. This could very well be the last time mother and son would see each other.

When it was time to leave, Louis tried to pick up Jean from Lea's bed.

"NON!" cried Jean. "Moi je reste ici avec maman!"

Lea tried to explain to Jean that he could not stay. "You must go with Papa, Jean. You can't stay here. This place is for sick people and you are a strong and healthy boy. You must go."

And with that directive, young Jean listened. He headed out and held his tears until he left her room, when he began to cry uncontrollably.

As Louis and Jean exited the building, the sun beat down directly on the two of them as they headed back to the car. It was a hot and muggy day.

"Did you want to play outside for a bit, Jean? There are some big rocks for you to climb, if you'd like."

Jean continued to cry and shook his head. And so, they headed to the car, the child screaming in his father's arms. From the second floor balcony, Lea could hear her young son's wailing as clear as day. And she too began to cry uncontrollably.

CHAPTER 12

Fall 1933

By early September, tests confirmed that tuberculosis had also spread to Lea's lungs.

Louis continued to visit Lea at least once or twice a week. He continued to work for the railway on a part-time basis. The other days, he helped his brother Léon on the farm in Grande Clairière. Because of this, he spent more time seeing Jean than Maurice. His youngest child was further away, and time did not allow for Louis to see him much. It was consoling to know that he was in good hands.

Lea was barely awake most visits. By now, she was being given large doses of medication for pain. These pills also made her incoherent when she was awake. Long gone were the days where Louis and Lea would talk for hours on end. Barely a word would be said between them.

October 2, 1933

Chère Lea,

I am writing you a few lines to let you know that I don't think that I will be able to visit you this week. If I can't get there during the week, I will be sure to go with my mother on Sunday, as long as the weather is good.

The reason I didn't go visit you yesterday was because of the estate sale. I still had a few dollars on me so I bought eight dollars' worth of stuff.

We are all in good health here.

I am pretty sure that I will be able to go see you next Sunday.

I love you with all my heart,

Louis

P.S. I am alone to work on the farm this week. The helper is gone to cut wood with Jerome.

Louis was busy working both on the trains and helping his brother with harvesting. There was a lot of work to be done on the farm before winter. On this particular week, his brother Léon was called to Saskatchewan to help another family member, so Louis had to take over the work required on the farm. There was no way he could make it down to see Lea.

He hoped to make it to Ninette the following Sunday. He wanted to let Lea know that he was able to purchase a few of Maman's items at the estate sale. He managed to buy a few pieces of her jewellery, a water vase, a washing board, a silver frying pan, and a trunk to hold all of these items. Surely, he could store this at Léon's until he found a place of his own. Everything he now owned fit in a two foot by three foot trunk.

Louis made it to Ninette on Sunday, October ninth. Lea was barely conscious. He spoke to her the entire time he was there, but barely got any responses from her. He told her that the boys were well taken care of and were doing well. He told her that he missed her so much, but that she shouldn't worry about him. He told her that whatever happened, he will be fine by himself, and that perhaps, if he prayed hard enough, this would all be over soon. He told her that he wished it was him that was going through this pain. He told her life was sometimes unfair. He told her how very much he loved her.

Before Louis left, he told Lea that she would soon receive a document to sign—her last will and testament. It was required that this be signed so that Louis and the two boys would receive what was rightfully theirs upon her death. Somehow, on October eleventh, Lea found the strength to sign her name.

Emaciated by her illness, Lea Mahy died on the evening of October 13, 1933. She was alone in her room at the time. No doctors, no nurses, no visitors. Louis was notified immediately.

Arrangements were made to take Lea back home, back with her loved ones in Grande Clairière.

Lea was buried on October sixteenth in the Grande Clairière cemetery, just across the road from where she and Louis had lived. Her tombstone is made of grey tyndall stone and is in the shape of a cross. It bears an image of a heart, signifying the love she had for her husband and children, and a rosary, which helped her through her darkest days.

Almost a year to the day since she was admitted to Souris Hospital, Lea Mahy was released from the pain and sorrow she had to endure. She was once again with her mother, who led her into the loving arms of God.

EPILOGUE

In 1928, a Scottish biologist named Alexander Fleming unintentionally discovered that when mold was presented in a pure culture, it had the ability to kill a number of disease-causing bacteria. This incident lead to the isolation of a substance called penicillium notanum. Fleming published his findings in a British Journal in 1929, and over the course of the next few years, continued to investigate his findings and work towards the development of an antibiotic.

Unfortunately, over time, he became frustrated with the process and shelved his research in 1931. It was not until 1940, when Oxford researchers Howard Florey and Ernst Boris Chain revived the project, that the substance was synthesized into a stable form of penicillin. Several clinical trials ensued, and by 1944, penicillin was being mass produced and distributed. In 1945, Fleming, Florey, and Chain received the Nobel Prize for their outstanding achievement in medical advances. Penicillin has saved, and continues to save lives of millions of people across the globe.

Alexander Fleming's discovery was the start of other antibiotic discoveries, including drugs such as Streptomycin and Isonicotinic, which are used in the fight against tuberculosis. Today, antibiotics are routinely used following surgeries such as appendectomies.

It is sad to think that Lea Mahy may not have died, nor might she have spent the last year of her life in hospital, away from her family, had these discoveries been produced sooner. Based on Lea's letters, she was never diagnosed with intestinal tuberculosis. Because her death certificate names Tuberculous Peritonitis as the main cause of death, and Pulmonary Tuberculosis as the contributory cause, we have to assume that she was diagnosed only in late May or early June. This would not have occurred in to today's world. The diagnosis would have come much sooner. Lea simply fell through the cracks.

By no means is Lea's story exclusive. Illness and disease took away many, many people in the early twentieth century. What is unique about Lea's story is that she recorded her experience via her letters. From these precious hand-written pieces of paper, her family was able to understand what she went through, how she handled the situation, and what she was like as a person.

Lea's dream to keep her family together did not materialize. Again, the times dictated this fate. Nowadays, people rarely die from appendectomies.

Medical procedures and testing are much more precise. Philosophies on the effects of diet and exercise have changed drastically. It is unlikely that any patient with intestinal issues would freely be given large meals, wine and chocolate while in a hospital. But this was the 1930s and times were different. Her family both understands and accepts that.

After Lea's death, Louis continued to live temporarily with various members of his family and friends. In 1934, his brother, Léon, moved his family to another small Manitoba town, so Louis, his mother, and young Jean moved into Léon's house in Grande Clairière. After a year, Léon and his family returned, Marie Mahy moved to Saskatchewan, and Louis and young Jean moved in with his father-in-law, Joseph Charles.

At some point, he was no longer able to care for his son. Young Jean moved back in with Léon and Palmyre, and they raised him until he was seventeen, when he went off to live on his own. Baby Maurice remained with his aunt Roseanna. She and her husband raised him until he became an adult.

Louis faced some tough times following Lea's death. He was financially strapped for many years. There is evidence that he was still unable to pay doctors' bills years after Lea had died. In a letter he wrote to a relative in 1940, he states:

> ... I don't have any money to send you... I
> could borrow some money and send it to
> you... I have $50, but I have to dress myself
> and the children with that... I haven't earned
> one cent since November 1939.

For years, he barely scraped by, living with family and friends and didn't ever really settle down in one particular town. He did eventually return to work full time for Canadian National Railway, but not until sometime in the 1940s.

Lea was the only one to have Louis' heart. When she died, he suffered a pain that time would never heal. He never remarried. He spent a lot of time on his own. He drank a lot. He saw his boys only occasionally. He did not take good care of himself. He did not live a long life. He died in 1961, from cancer, at the age of sixty-five.

Lea's letters, held in a tattered pink, floral box that originally held chocolates, were kept by her mother Sylvie until her untimely death in May, 1933. At that time, it is presumed that they were taken and cared for by Lea's sister Palmyre. Because Louis wandered from place to place to live, he asked that they be held in safekeeping. For years, they were placed in a trunk that held his only possessions and remained at Léon and Palmyre's home. Palmyre gave them to Jean after Louis passed away. This was the first time Jean had seen the letters. He held them for a number of years and eventually passed them on to his brother Maurice.

It is gratifying to know that both Jean and Maurice lived long and healthy lives. At the time of writing, both are well into their eighties. Both grew up hearing only the odd story about their mother, but both knew from her letters that she thought about them every day and loved them both very much. Still, this is a small consolation for growing up without their mother.

From the testimony of Lea's family members and from her expressive and heartrending letters, we get a good picture of who Lea Mahy was. Loving wife, caring mother. She was a hard-working, family-oriented woman with a persevering nature. For the most part, she kept a positive attitude throughout her illness and encouraged her husband to do the same. She loved her young sons with all her heart and made sure they knew this every time she picked up a pencil. Sadly, she was taken from her loved ones much too soon.

ACKNOWLEDGEMENTS

First of all, this book would not have been possible without the permission of the Mahy family to include Lea's letters. These letters are the crux of the story.

Before writing this book, I first had to translate the letters. I had excellent help from none other than one of my sisters, Claudette. Her French language skills are impeccable, and she was very helpful in finding the precise word in so many instances. Thank you also to my sister Denise for reading snippets of this book over the past three years, and being brutally honest about what worked and what didn't. I also enjoyed spending the day with you and Joe, as we explored Souris, Hartney, Grande Clairière and the grounds of the Ninette Sanatorium.

Much of the background came from a book entitled *Settlers, Sand and Steeple: Grande Clairière and District 1888-1988*. This book was published by the parish of St. John in Grande Clairière to commemorate the one-hundredth anniversary of the town, and is filled with story after story of the many families who inhabited Grande Clairière since its beginnings. This publication was invaluable to me in putting together Lea's story.

Though much of the infrastructure at the Ninette Sanatorium is no longer there, a few buildings are still standing. Thank you to the present owner of this parcel of land, Ronnie Aschenbrenner, for allowing us on the grounds and inside the administration building to peruse at our leisure on a fine fall day. Everything from the furniture and artwork, to the medical paraphernalia to the recipes in the kitchen, helped me to describe what life in Ninette was like in 1933.

One of my biggest surprises when researching this book was the expansive train system that existed in the 1930s. Most towns in Manitoba were serviced by a railroad line; some had two lines that ran through it. Much of this information was found online, but a key helper was Peter Lacey, who is assistant archivist at the Winnipeg Railway Museum. I was amazed that he still had schedules and other documents that outlined time-tables and pricing.

Others who helped us to with background information include Sarah Ramsden at the City of Winnipeg Archives and staff at the Manitoba Archives. I was able to get some good information about electricity in the 1930s, and would like to thank Kim Larcombe at the Manitoba Electrical Museum for this. We also came across some interesting exhibits at the Souris and Hartney Museums.

This helped me paint an accurate picture of life in rural Manitoba in the 1930s.

I was also fortunate to have the help of two friends with medical backgrounds—Fisayo Akinseye and Gisele Hansen—look over my manuscript and help me with correct terminology for the medical information I included.

A huge thank you everyone at FriesenPress who was involved with the making of my book. As a newcomer to this process, you helped me to weave through the various steps and come up with a great final product. I truly appreciated your input on editing, formatting, layout and design. A special thank you to my brother-in-law Doug who was able to touch up the photo shown on the outside back cover.

To those closest to me—John, Lisa, Lori, David, Ryan, Carolyn, Ethan, Ava, Jackson, Claudette, Lorraine, Louise, Denise, Cindy, Hélène —you've heard me talk about this book for the last four years. I've read different parts to each of you and asked all of you for your opinion at one time or another. Thank you all so much for your constant support and enthusiasm.

Last, but certainly not least, thank you to the Mahy family:

Joe—for the countless hours of researching, reviewing, revising, editing and discussing what stays and what goes. For writing the foreword and for so often finding the just the right word to use, as we read and reread the manuscript. (dinner vs supper... who knew?)You have been a rock throughout this whole process and I couldn't have done it without you.

To his wife, Michelle—for the massive amount of research you amassed for me over the years, and for taking many, many photos to find the perfect one for the cover. And, at the last minute, for coming up with the ideal pencil graphic to place before each of Lea's letters... thank you. How special that I got to work with one of my favourite relatives!

To Dave and Val—for taking the time to review and revise these pages at various times over the last few years, helping me with my research (our little trip to Hartney,Val!), and for meeting with me when I went to visit Grande Clairière.

To Aurélie Gagnon and Eva Critchley—as descendants of Palmyre and Léon, you were instrumental in giving me a great glimpse of your family traditions. Thank you for sharing many incredible memories; much of what you shared ended up in this book.

To Lorraine and Marie Mahy—I was so pleased to meet you both. As spouses of Jean and Maurice, I can see how this tragic part of your husbands' lives has also touched your own. In both of you, I could see the genuine love and affection you have for your husbands, as they recalled what they could about their past.

And most especially, to Jean and Maurice Mahy— words cannot express how grateful I am to have been given the opportunity to meet you both and to write this book. Your mother was a remarkable woman—I knew it the moment I started reading her letters. She made me cry, she made me laugh, she broke my heart. She loved you both immensely and I thank you from the bottom of my heart for letting me share her letters and this story with the rest of the world.

Printed in Canada